First Reader

First Reader

by Phyllis Schlafly

with illustrations by Elaine Atkinson

Pere Marquette Press
Alton, Illinois

Phyllis Schlafly spent many years developing this curriculum, beginning with teaching her own six children to read during the 1950s and 1960s. It is based on three premises:

1:   that any parent can teach a child to read, regardless of the educational level attained by the parent;

2:   that the home, not the school, is the best place for children to learn to read, because reading is a solitary, not a social, activity; and

3:   that the best way to achieve the number-one goal of U.S. education policy — "Every child should start school ready to learn" — is for parents to teach their children to read **before** they enter school.

Mrs. Schlafly, B.A., M.A., J.D., LL.D. (hon.), is the author or co-author of 16 books.

Elaine Atkinson is a graphic designer living in Lubbock, Texas.

Published by
Pere Marquette Press Inc.
P. O. Box 495
Alton, Illinois 62002

Library of Congress Catalog Card Number 93-087484

ISBN 0-934640-24-6

Printed in the United States of America

10 9 8 7 6 5 4 3 2 1

Foreword

First Reader is "User-Friendly." This means it is easy for the child *and* the teacher to use.

First Reader is Child-Friendly. It is written especially for children **before** they enter school. That's why it uses big print and many words selected for children. Children who learn what is in this book will be able to read — and will have started on the road to a good education. They will fulfill today's Number One National Education Goal: "Every child should start school ready to learn."

Nothing will give a child such a sense of achievement — earned self-esteem! — as mastering the skill of unlocking sounds and syllables so he can read words, then sentences, then a story, and then a book. It is important to use *First Reader* **before** the child is taught wrong habits, such as pretending to "read" by looking at pictures, guessing what is in the text, or memorizing a story.

First Reader is also Teacher-Friendly. The teacher does not have to study a lot of instructions because this book is written in a logical and straightforward way. You will be surprised at how little time it takes to teach a child to read. It can easily be accomplished even by a mother or father employed fulltime outside of the home.

First Reader is designed for one child to be taught by one older person who cares a lot about that child — a mother, a father, a grandmother, a grandfather, or other relative or friend. We'll call this person the "Reading Teacher." This person does not have to have a college degree or any special training. The Reading Teacher just has to follow these ten rules:

1. Sound out each new page. The purpose of the pictures is to help the child learn and remember the proper sounds. It is important to pronounce each sound correctly. The pictures in this book do not tell a

story; they do not represent words or situations. The pictures represent sounds that the child must learn in order to read.

2. Study the pages in order, and have the child master each page perfectly before moving to another page. Don't skip around. *First Reader* is designed so that a child can progress from page to page in a rational way. The sequence of the pages is very important. The child should learn each page completely before moving on to the next page. When you start, it is normal for the child to spend several days on each page before moving to the next page. Each day, the child should review the pages he already learned.

3. Teach the reading lessons in 20-minute segments. Don't try to hold a child to the book longer than 20 minutes at a time; if you do, the child will become tired and discouraged. I suggest no more than three 20-minute segments a day, with recess periods of at least 10 minutes in between the segments. Try to use a quiet room without other distractions (such as music). Be sure to have a good light on the book.

4. Some children learn best with a regular time and place for the lessons. Others do well when the lessons are at different times of the day to accommodate the Reading Teacher's schedule. Some children learn best when they sit up at a child's table, chair, or desk. Others do better sitting cozily on the sofa next to the Reading Teacher. "It is important that the lessons be a warm and loving one-on-one experience."

5. Do not tell a child that learning to read is "play," "fun," a "game," or "entertainment." Do not let the child expect to see images jumping around as they do on television. Learning to read is an adventure in which the child learns to decode the **written symbols** which correspond to the **spoken words** the child already knows. (A 5-year-old has a speaking vocabulary of many thousands of words.)

6. The Reading Teacher must have patience. Children learn at different speeds. Don't nag. Let each child go at his own pace. Teaching a child *First Reader* can take anywhere from two months to six months or longer, and it can be used at any age. (Age 5 is typical.) How long it

takes a child to go through *First Reader* — or at what age he starts — has almost nothing to do with how smart the child is. But studying the entire book completely **before** he is taught by any other method will have everything to do with how well the child will learn later — because *First Reader* teaches good reading habits and provides the tools to enable the child eventually to read anything he or she wants to read.

7. The Reading Teacher must have enthusiasm. Learning to read should be exciting for both teacher and child. Make each lesson an important daily event. Give the child praise and rewards when he reads a page perfectly. It may be a couple of months before you discover the excitement, but it will be a real thrill the first time a child sounds out a long word, such as "grasshopper," all by himself. The only other child's achievement that is as thrilling to child and parent is learning to walk!

8. Learning to read is a solitary exercise, not a group activity. That's why it is difficult for a child to learn to read in a classroom. Learning to read is like learning to walk, to ride a bicycle, or to play the piano. You have to do it by yourself. If two children begin at the same time, they should be taught separately to ensure that each learns at his own pace.

9. *First Reader Workbook* should be used as a companion to *First Reader* so the child can write the letters he learns each day. Writing the letters is a tremendous help in learning to recognize the sounds and syllables. *First Reader* and *First Reader Workbook* are not filled up with unnecessary words or boring "busy work" to tire out the child. Useless "busy work" is what children are forced to do in school when reading is taught in a class. That's why some small children get school "burn-out" without learning how to read.

10. The Reading Teacher should read the Ears and Eyes page to the child before starting. The Reading Teacher should read the Lesson Instructions at the end of this book before teaching each page.

Phyllis Schlafly

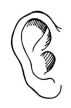 The ear means: Sound out each word and listen to its sound.

 The eye means: You must see these words with your eye and remember them.

 A hand behind the ear means: These words go by a different rule, so listen more closely with your ear.

 A hand over the eye means: You expect to see the letter "e," but it is not there. You can't see it.

 The ears covered with hands mean: Some letters are silent. You can't hear them at all when you say the words.

 Sometimes you see a letter one way,

 but you hear a different sound when you say the word.

a
A

u
U

i
I

3

O
o

e
E

m
M

ma	mu	mi	mo	me
man	mud	miss	mop	met
mad	mum	mitt	mops	men
mat	mug	mill	mob	mess
map	mutt	Mick	moss	Meg
mass	muff	in	Mom	
Matt	muss		on	
	up			

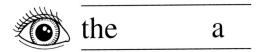

the   a

Mick met Meg on the mat.

Mom mops up the mess.

Matt met a man in the mud.

S
S

8

sa	su	si	so	se
sat	sun	sit	sob	set
sad	sum	sip	sod	sell
sap	sub	sin	sop	send
Sam	suck	sick	Sol	sent
sand		Sis	on	
Sal		Sid		
		in		
		is		

the

Sam sits on the sand.

Sis and Sal sat in the sun.

Sid is sad in the sub.

r
R

ra	ru	ri	ro	re
rap	run	rid	rob	red
ran	rub	rip	rod	rep
ram	rug	rig	rot	reg
rat	rut	rib	rock	rent
rack	rust	rim	Ron	
Ann			Rob	
at			on	

from	a	the	had

Rob ran from Ron.

Ann sat on a red rug.

The rat ran at Ron.

The rag rug had a rip.

p
P

pa	pu	pi	po	pe
pan	pup	pig	pot	pet
pat	pug	pin	pop	pen
pap	pun	pit	pod	pep
pad	pus	pip	Pol	peck
pass	puff	pill	pond	Peg
Pam	putt	pick		
Pat	pump	is		
and	puck	in		
	up			

a	2	has

Mom has a pot and a pan.

Pat has 2 pets — a pup and a pig.

The pig is up in a pen.

Pam and Peg pet the pup.

f

F

fa	fu	fi	fo	fe
fat	fun	fit	fog	fed
fan	fuss	fib	fob	fell
fad	fuzz	fin	off	fend
fast		fig		
and		fill		
		fish		
		if		

a	to	the	has	with

Pam fed a fig to the fat pig.

Pat has fun with the fan.

Rob has a fish with fins.

Sis fell off the rock.

d
D

16

da	du	di	do	de
dam	dug	did	dot	den
dab	dub	dig	doll	deck
Dad	dud	dip	dock	dell
Dan	dull	din	Don	desk
and	duck	dim	Dot	Ed
		Dick	odd	
		in	on	
		is	dog	

the	A	see	or

Dan and Dot dug in the mud.

Don met Dick in the den.

See the duck on the dock.

A doll is on the desk or the deck.

g
G

ga	gu	gi	go	ge
gab	gun	give	got	get
gag	gum	gift	gob	egg
gas	gut	gig	God	
gat	gull		golf	
gap	Gus			
	gust			

-ag	bag	lag	hag	sag
	nag	rag	tag	

his	from	of	?

Did Gus get his gas?

Dan got a gift from God.

Don got a gob of gum.

Did Gus give a rag doll to Dot?

ta	tu	ti	to	te
tan	tub	tin	tot	ten
tap	tug	tip	top	tell
tab	tut	till	toss	Ted
tad	tuck	tick	tock	Tess
tat	tuff	Tim	Tom	
tam		it	Todd	
Tad		if		
		tiff		

to	has	said	?	" "

Did Ted toss a red top to Tim?

Tess has ten tan tops in the tin tub.

Did Dad tell Mom to tuck Tom in bed?

Tad said, "Tick, tock, tick, tock."

b
B

ba	bu	bi	bo	be
bad	bus	big	box	bed
bag	bug	bit	bog	bet
bam	but	bib	boss	beg
ban	bun	bin	Bob	Ben
bat	buff	Bill	on	Bess
bass	bum	Biff		
Babs	Bud	in		
and	Buck			

the	said	I	had

Ben bit the bun in the bag.

Bob and Bud met on the bus.

But Bill said, "I had a big bat."

Bess had a bad bug in the box.

n
N

na	nu	ni	no	ne
nap	nut	nip	not	net
nab	nub	nit	nod	neck
nag	nun	nib	nob	Ned
Nan		Nick	nog	Nell
Nat			on	

in	pin	tin	din	fin	bin

has	to	had	his

Nan has a nut in a net.

Did Dad nag Nick to nap on the bed?

Ned had a bib on his neck.

Nell has a pin in a tin box.

c
C

k
K

ca	cu	ki	co	ke
cat	cup	kit	cot	keg
can	cub	kid	cop	Ken
can't	cut	kick	con	Kent
cab	cud	Kim	cob	keds
cap	cuff	kiss	cock	kept
cad		kill	cod	
Cass			cog	
Cal				

-ck

-ack	-uck	-ick	-ock	-eck
sack	suck	kick	sock	neck
back	duck	sick	tock	peck
pack	tuck	pick	rock	deck
rack	puck	tick	cock	
tack	buck	Dick	dock	
hack		Nick	mock	

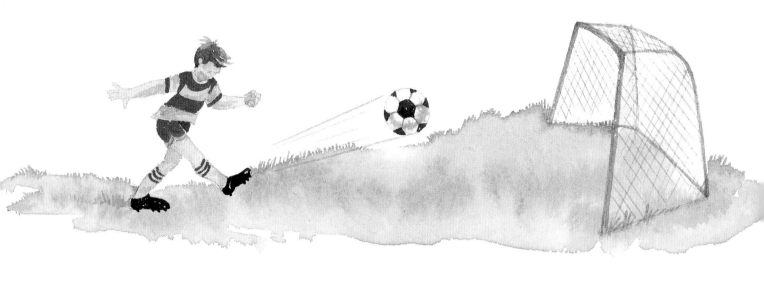

Can Mack pack a sack?

Rock can kick the can to Kent.

Mom can kiss Dad.

Dick is sick in bed.

Tick, tock, tick, tock.

Cass is in a cab with Nick.

Rick can pick up a red sock.

Kim has a cat, not a cub.

Mack has a duck, not a kid.

The duck has a big neck.

The cat has a big back.

ma	gu	ne	ri	tu
fo	pe	su	de	ca
si	ro	be	ga	bi
gas	cod	is	bit	sun
Gus	cob	if	bet	Sam
did	gun	in	cat	red
Dad	gum	it	fat	rat
Ed	bad	on	Don	tap
Ted	bed	off	Dan	pat
pet	ten	egg	set	pet
pat	tan	odd	sin	Pam
Mom	rug	has	Dick	nap
mop	ran	had	Nick	pan
can	bag	up	not	kick
cup	tug	at	Nan	back

the	a	from	had	to
has	with	see	or	his
of	said	I	off	on

29

h
H

30

ha	hu	hi	ho	he
hat	hug	hit	hot	hen
ham	hub	him	hop	hem
has	hum	his	hob	hell
had	hut	hip	hod	help
hand	hull	hid	hog	
have	huff	hill	hock	
Hal	up	it	on	
Hank				

Can the hen hop up the hill?

Has Hank his hat in his hand?

I have a ham, but Ben hid it.

Is the hog in the hut?

Did the pig huff and puff?

Did Hal help Bob get the hen?

l
L

la	lu	li	lo	le
lad	lug	lit	lot	let
lag	luck	lip	log	led
lap	lump	lid	loss	leg
last		lick	lost	less
lamp			lock	lend
land				

-el	tell	sell	bell	fell	Nell
-il	hill	sill	fill	dill	Bill

Did Bill let the cat lick his leg?

The lad has a lump on his lip.

Tell Dad to lock the lid.

The cat sat on the lap of Dan.

Nell had bad luck. Nell fell on the bell.

Can Bill sell the doll to the lass?

34

ja	ju	ji	jo	je
jam	jump	jig	job	jet
jag	jut	Jim	jot	jell
Jack	just	Jill	jog	Jeff
jacks	jug	jib	Jon	Jess
Jan	up			jest

down	see	go	with	from

Did Jeff just jump up and down?

Can Jon see the jet go up or down?

Jan can get a job with Jim.

Can Jack and Jill jog up the hill

to get a jug of jam?

Did Jess get his jacks from Tom?

wa	wi	we
wag	win	wet
wags	wig	web
	wit	well
	with	welt
	wilt	wend
	wind	went

Will went with the west wind.

The wet bug is in the web.

qua	qui	que
quack	quit	quest
	quick	quell
	quill	
	quilt	
	quip	

"Quack, quack," said the quick duck.

Will Jeff jump on the quilt?

V
v

X
X

va	vi	ve
van	vim	vet
vat	Vic	vend
vamp		vent
vast		vest
Val		

Val ran to the van.

Vic has a wet vest.

-ax	-ix	-ox	-ex
ax	mix	ox	vex
sax	six	box	hex
tax	fix	fox	
lax	nix	pox	
wax			
Max			

Did the fox see Bob wax the red van?

Jim will mix six jacks in the box.

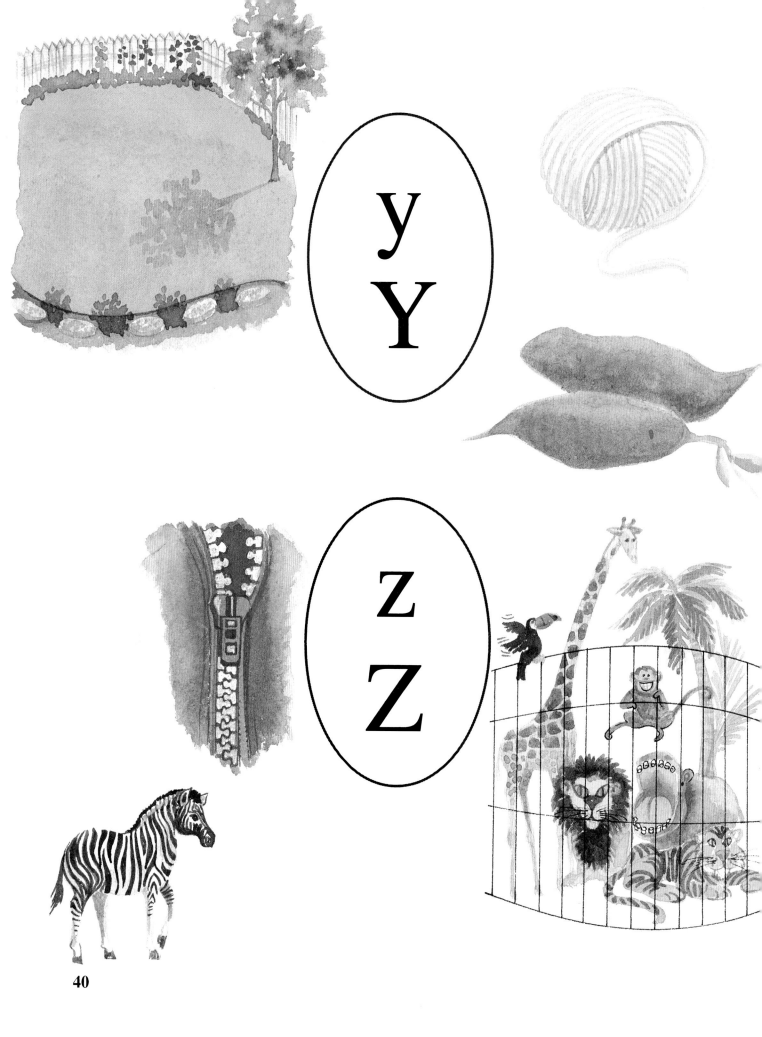

y
Y

z
Z

40

ya	yu	yi	yo	ye
yam	yuck	yip	yon	yes
yak	us			yet
yap				yen
				yell
				yelp

Ben will yell and Lad will yelp.

Yes, yes, Mom will help us.

za	zi	ze	-z	-zz
zap	zip	zest	quiz	jazz
zag	zig	Zed	Liz	buzz
Zack			Oz	fuzz
			Roz	fizz

Did Zack pass his quiz?

The bug with fuzz said "Buzz."

	pan	pant	pants	
pan	cut	mill	sand	Mom
pant	cuts	milk	hand	Mom's
ten	muss	men	lamp	Dad
tent	must	mend	camp	Dad's
tin	miss	sill	mat	Ben
tint	mist	silk	mats	Ben's
Gus	send	bell	men	Jack
gust	sent	belt	mess	Jack's
bus	and	ten	duck	Ann
bust	ant	tend	ducks	Ann's
sell	pass	fun	ban	Meg
self	past	fuss	band	Meg's
hum	give	fell	dam	Tom
hump	gift	felt	damp	Tom's
bell	bum	puff	wag	Kim
belt	bump	puffs	wags	Kim's

zig	big	ham	Max	vest
zag	bad	hum	fix	vast
zip	bug	hem	fox	vend
tick	pack	rock	duck	sock
tock	pick	rack	dock	sick
tack	puck	Rick	Dick	sack
quick	wig	Jim	lock	hill
quack	wag	jam	luck	hell
quest	wet	jump	lack	Hal
lump	doll	Jack	yap	less
lamp	dill	Jill	yip	lass
lend	dell	Jeff	yelp	list
jazz	fox	puff	bend	rub
buzz	mix	cuff	band	rib
quiz	tax	huff	bond	rag

down	go	see	with	said
in	is	up	of	if

sh
Sh

sha	shu	shi	sho	she
shad	shut	ship	shop	shed
shall	shun	shill	shot	shell
shack	shuck	shin	shock	shelf
sham	shush	shift		
shaft				

-ash	-ush	-ish
dash	gush	dish
mash	mush	fish
gash	hush	wish
rash	rush	
hash	brush	

Kim has a dish of fish on the ship.

Matt shall rush to the shop to get a fish.

Is the shell on the sand or on the shelf?

Is the hash in the shed or in the shack?

ch
Ch

cha	chu	chi	cho	che
chat	chug	chick	chop	check
chap	chum	chip	chock	chess
champ	chump	chill	chomp	chest
chant	Chuck	chin		Chet

	-uch	-ich	
	much	rich	ostrich
	such	sandwich	

-atch	-utch	-itch	-otch	-etch
catch	Dutch	hitch	botch	fetch
batch	hutch	pitch	notch	ketch
hatch	crutch	ditch	scotch	retch
patch	clutch	witch		
match				

-nch	-nch	-nch	-nch
ranch	lunch	inch	bench
	punch	pinch	quench
	bunch	clinch	clench
	hunch	finch	
	munch		

ch   -ch   -tch

 her   so   his   he   she

I have a hunch the fox will catch the chick.

Will the hen hatch eggs so we can have lunch?

Chuck will sit on a bench and win at chess.

Chad has a patch on his pants.

Jack, Ned and Tim are a bunch of chums.

Dan will pitch the tent and have so much fun.

He will not botch the job.

Sal will get the cat from the ditch.

She will dash back and Dan will not catch her.

It is a shock to see the chimp in the shop.

la	lu	li	lo	le
sla	slu	sli	slo	sle
slap	slum	slip	slot	sled
slab	slump	slid	slop	slept
slam	slug	slim	slob	
slack	slush	slit	slosh	
slash		slick		
slant				

la	lu	li	lo	le
cla	clu	cli	clo	cle
clam	club	clip	clod	clef
clap	cluck	cliff	clot	clench
clamp	clump	click	clog	
class	clutch	clinch	clop	
clash			clock	

la	lu	li	lo	le
bla	blu	bli	blo	ble
black	blush	bliss	block	bled
bland	blunt	blimp	blot	bless
blast	bluff	blitz	blond	blest
blanch			blob	blend

la	lu	li	lo	le
pla	plug	li	plo	ple
plan	pluck	pli	plot	pled
plant	plum	plim	plop	
plat	plump	plinth	plod	
	plus			
	plush			

la	lu	li	lo	le
fla	flu	fli	flo	fle
flat	flub	flick	flog	fled
flag	fluff	flit	flop	fleck
flash	flush	flint	flock	flesh
flap		flip	floss	flex

la	lu	li	lo	le
gla	glu	gli	glo	gle
glad	glum	glib	glob	glen
glass	glut	glint	gloss	Glenn
gland		glim		

pa	pu	pi	po	pe
spa	spu	spi	spo	sped
spat	spun	spin	spot	spell
span	spud	spit	Spock	speck
		spill		spend
				spent

ca	cu	ki	co	ke
sca	scu	ski	sco	ske
scat	scuff	skip	scot	sketch
scan	scud	skin	scotch	
scab	scum	skit	scoff	
scalp	skull	skid	Scott	
scant		skim		

na	nu	ni	no	ne
sna	snu	sni	sno	sne
snap	snug	snip	snob	snell
snag	snub	sniff		
snack	snuff	snick		

51

ma	mu	mi	mo	me
sma	smu	smi	smo	sme
smack	smug	Smith	smog	smell
smash			smock	smelt

wa	wu	wi	wo	we
swa	swu	swi	swo	swe
swag	swum	swim	swob	swell
swam		swift		swept
		swish		

ta	tu	ti	to	te
sta	stu	sti	sto	ste
stack	stub	still	stop	step
stamp	stuck	stick	stock	stem
stand	stump	stiff	stomp	stuff

tra	tru	tri	tro	tre
rap	rut	rip	rop	rep
trap	strut	trip	strop	strep
strap	struck	strip		
strand	strum			

you　　　your　　　come　　　he

See the flag on the glass stand.

Can you spell Mom and Dad?

Gwen said, "God bless you."

Will the clock stop if you smash it?

Can you clench your fist and snap your hands?

Come and see Bob Smith's flock of chicks.

Scott is glad he has a slick black sled.

Glenn slept on a slab at the bluff.

Mick swam fast to the stump on the cliff.

Cliff had a blot of ink on his quiz.

Mitch fell on the step and his leg bled.

I will pluck a plump plum from the stem.

fact	dusk	lift	golf	left
raft	just	gift	romp	desk
gasp	must	list	last	next
last	rust	quilt	gasp	text
camp	bulb	film	went	best
task	gulf	swift	wind	west
sent	hump	quick	clock	self
bent	dump	risk	blond	help
land	milk	mend	block	belt
scalp	silk	melt	flock	slept
sand	jump	can't	stomp	kept
send	bump	clinch	scotch	chest
go	he	she	I	so
from	down	said	her	come

cap	fat	mat	Sal	can
cape	fate	mate	sale	cane
tap	pan	sham	mad	Sam
tape	pane	shame	made	same
back	rack	sack	tack	shack
bake	rake	sake	take	shake
Tam	fad	pal	man	hat
tame	fade	pale	mane	hate
quack	lack	flam	plat	lack
quake	lake	flame	plate	lake
plan	stack	slat	snack	Jan
plane	stake	slate	snake	Jane
came	late	make	gaze	save
game	gate	cake	daze	safe

55

hid	rid	kit	bit	Tim
hide	ride	kite	bite	time
fill	pin	lick	rip	din
file	pine	like	ripe	dine
Dick	pick	shin	fin	till
dike	pike	shine	fine	tile
sit	dim	pill	mitt	mill
site	dime	pile	mite	mile
Mick	snip	Sid	pick	spin
Mike	snipe	side	pike	spine
slid	still	spin	spick	back
slide	stile	spine	spike	bake
life	five	wide	mine	dive
wife	nine	tide	lime	smile

cub	duck	tub	cut	dun
cube	duke	tube	cute	dune
Jock	not	doll	rob	rub
joke	note	dole	robe	Rube
rod	cock	con	pock	dot
rode	coke	cone	poke	dote
cop	mop	lob	glob	Spock
cope	mope	lobe	globe	spoke
slop	rot	smock	stock	mod
slope	rote	smoke	stoke	mode
sole	home	bone	stone	woke
mole	hole	lone	tone	choke

Eve	Pete	Steve

The jet plane will shine and glide.

Dale will come home at five o'clock.

I hope God will bless your home.

Jane will bake a cake and Kate will taste it.

Duke kept his date on time.

Blake will rake on the hill in the shade.

Will haste make waste?

James will wake up late at nine o'clock.

Pete will take home a fine black slate.

Eve has a dime to spend at the store.

Can Luke ride his bike on the slope?

old	no	kind	blind
bold	go	find	child
cold	so	hind	wild
fold	lo	bind	mild
gold	fro	mind	

hold	most	rind
mold	almost	wind
sold	post	grind
told	gross	

I told you to hold on to your hat.

The old man said, "It is so cold."

Let us be kind to the blind child.

Dan sold most of his gold.

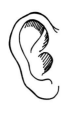 

cat	run	flit	hop	shell
cats	runs	flits	hops	shells

sack	duck	ride	rock	sled
sacks	ducks	rides	rocks	sleds

ship	jump	pop	bed	check
ships	jumps	pops	beds	checks

plane	grape	duke	smile	joke
planes	grapes	dukes	smiles	jokes

Dad	Buck	Dick	Mom	Meg
Dad's	Buck's	Dick's	Mom's	Meg's

Jack	Kim	Dot	Jeff	Gus
Jack's	Kim's	Dot's	Jeff's	Gus's

Jake	Mike	Kate	Duke	Pete
Jake's	Mike's	Kate's	Duke's	Pete's

ra	ru	ri	ro	re
tra	tru	tri	tro	tre
trap	truck	trip	trot	tress
track	trump	Rick	rod	trek
ramp	Russ	trick	trod	trend
tramp	truss	rim		
trash	trust	trim		

ra	ru	ri	ro	re
cra	cru	cri	cro	cre
rack	rust	crib	crop	rest
crack	crust	rim	rock	crest
crab	rush	crimp	crock	crept
cramp	crush	crisp	cross	
crass	crux	crick	crotch	
crash	crunch			

ra	ru	ri	ro	re
fra	fru	fri	fro	fre
Fran	frump	rill	from	fresh
Frank		frill	frog	fret
		risk	frock	Fred
		frisk	frost	French

ra	ru	ri	ro	re
dra	dru	dri	dro	dre
rag	rum	drip	drop	dress
drag	drum	drill		drench
drab	rug	drift		
draft	drug			

ra	ra	ru	ri	ro
gra	gra	gru	rip	gro
grab	grab	ruff	grip	grog
grass	raft	gruff	rim	
gram	graft	rub	grim	Greg
grand	rasp	grub	grid	
grant	grasp	runt	grin	
grad	grand	grunt	grill	

ra	ru	ri	ri	re
bra	bru	bri	rig	bre
brag	rush	brim	brig	red
bran	brush	risk	Rick	bred
brand	brunt	brisk	brick	Brett
ranch	brunch	rink	brim	Brent
branch		brink		
brass				

no	you	eye	want	for
do	your	see	come	to

Brad made a trip in a black truck.

Did the truck crash on the track?

No, it fell in the trench, but Brad is safe.

Fran will print your name on the drum.

Come and see Fred do a trick with his eye.

Do you want a dress or a frock for Priss?

Will you be still? The babe is in the crib.

I trust Greg to grill the fresh fish for us.

Is the frog on the raft or the branch?

| brag | brim | grand | crop | dress |
| drag | prim | brand | prop | press |

| trick | crust | crimp | crock | brunch |
| brick | trust | primp | frock | crunch |

| draft | cramp | crush | drum | trim |
| craft | tramp | brush | trump | grim |

Can Brett rake the grass in the grove?

Will the trash drift on the grass?

Can Brent drive his prize to trade it?

Yes, Brent drove his grand prize to the gate.

You are brave to ride with Steve.

Greg will grab the crab and crack it.

Fritz has a crate of grapes in the cave.

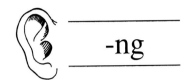 -ng

sang	sung	sing	gong
rang	rung	wing	pong
bang	bung	ping	dong
hang	hung	king	song
pang	lung	sling	long
gang	stung	ring	belong
fang	swung	bring	strong
clang	strung	string	
sprang	sprung	spring	

Bing sang a song for the gang.

Jeff swung Roz in the swing.

Ding, dong, rang the clock.

Ping pong is a fun game.

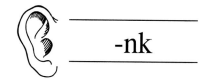

-nk

bank	sunk	sink	pink
blank	dunk	stink	rink
tank	junk	wink	drink
sank	bunk	link	brink
rank	drunk	clink	blink
drank	skunk	slink	shrink
frank	slunk		
prank	chunk		

spank	plank	flank	clank
spunk	plunk	flunk	clunk

Come and see the skunk on the grass.

Frank had a drink from the tank.

Honk if you want to skate at the rink.

Hank's junk is on the bunk.

The dimes went clink-clank in my bank.

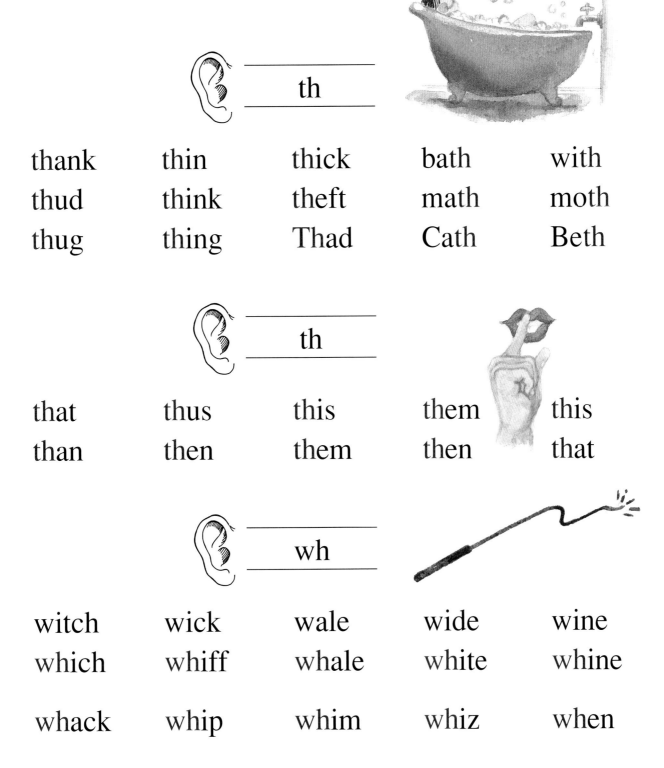

th				
thank	thin	thick	bath	with
thud	think	theft	math	moth
thug	thing	Thad	Cath	Beth

th				
that	thus	this	them	this
than	then	them	then	that

wh				
witch	wick	wale	wide	wine
which	whiff	whale	white	whine
whack	whip	whim	whiz	when

Cath will do her math with Beth.

I think Mom is with Dad.

When will that whale take a bath?

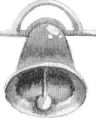

clap	hum	win	hop
clapping	humming	winning	hopping
kill	buzz	dig	mop
killing	buzzing	digging	mopping
nap	puff	pin	rob
napping	puffing	pinning	robbing
stand	run	hit	pop
standing	running	hitting	popping
catch	jump	fish	rock
catching	jumping	fishing	rocking
plant	rub	dip	stop
planting	rubbing	dipping	stopping
drag	cluck	skip	drop
dragging	clucking	skipping	dropping
tramp	fuss	swim	stock
tramping	fussing	swimming	stocking
beg	get	step	dress
begging	getting	stepping	dressing

 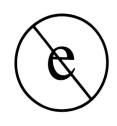

make	hide	joke	ride
making	hiding	joking	riding
take	shine	shake	skate
taking	shining	shaking	skating
name	like	doze	drive
naming	liking	dozing	driving
rake	smile	smoke	chase
raking	smiling	smoking	chasing
taste	swipe	slope	hike
tasting	swiping	sloping	hiking
paste	dine	mope	slide
pasting	dining	moping	sliding
trade	bite	poke	wake
trading	biting	poking	waking
grade	glide	hope	brake
grading	gliding	hoping	braking
blaze	blame	stone	quake
blazing	blaming	stoning	quaking

-nk	th	wh	-ing

who	why	what	where	want
come	you	she	for	do

Hank wants to go fishing with Chet.

Thad is stopping to get a tank of gas.

Honk if you want to come with them.

Beth will go swimming in the lake.

Who will go with her?

Why can't you go?

What time will she go?

Where is the lake?

Cath can't go. She has to do her math.

Seth said, "Thank you for not smoking."

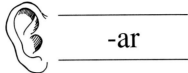 -ar

car	tar	far	are	bark
card	star	farm	arm	dark
lard	start	cart	barn	park
smart	chart	scar	yard	lark
march	sharp	scarf	hard	spark

Mark said, "Sharks do not live in lakes."

Bart went to the farm to see a barn.

Is Charles parking his car in the yard?

Marg got a scar on her arm in the dark.

Can Lars and Carl march to the park?

Barb is smart to start on her chart.

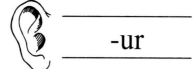

-ur

| burn | curl | surf | churn | fur |
| turn | hurt | turf | church | burp |

-ir

girl	sir	dirt	bird
third	stir	first	birth
Kirk	skirt	whirl	birch

-er

her	term	clerk	herb	Herb
herd	pert	berth	perch	Fern
verb	perk	term	Vern	Bert

Fern was the first girl to get hurt.

The nurse said it is a bad burn on her arm.

Barb wants the third skirt on the rack.

The bird on the branch will chirp at Vern.

72

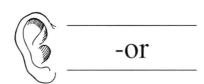

-or

horn	born	corn	for	fore
horse	torn	lord	fork	more
short	north	porch	pork	core
form	sort	scorch	storm	gore
morn	cork	stork	snort	sore

Norm has a horse in the barn.

The storm hit the porch in the morning.

Burt is smart to ride north, not west.

Kurt has a fork to stir his corn.

Is Fern riding a horse or a car?

Barb will not scorch the pork!

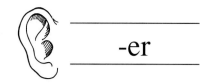 -er

mat	sum	big	lock	help
matter	summer	bigger	locker	helper
skate	cute	ride	joke	buzz
skater	cuter	rider	joker	buzzer
farm	curl	twirl	form	hard
farmer	curler	twirler	former	harder
lad	pitch	spin	rock	help
ladder	pitcher	spinner	rocker	helper
black	drum	win	corn	dress
blacker	drummer	winner	corner	dresser

The farmer has corn in the corner of his barn.

Will the drummer or the skater be the winner?

In the summer, we drive to the farm to have supper.

74

 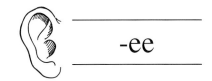 -ee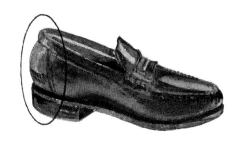

bee	tee	see	fee	heel
beet	tree	seen	feet	green
beef	free	seed	feel	Greek
week	weed	seem	feed	sleep
sheet	sweet	cheek	cheer	steel
sheep	sweep	sleet	sleeve	freeze
wheel	creep	greet	geese	cheese

Lee got stung on her cheek by a bee.

Do you see the golf tee by the big tree?

I have seen Reed greet his sweet Mom.

Do you feel as if your feet will freeze?

I can see three deer in the green weeds.

 be   me   he   she   we   been

75

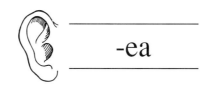

-ea

eat	beat	read	leaf	ear
each	seat	real	lead	fear
teach	heat	reach	leave	hear
beach	meat	peach	clean	dear
tea	ream	beast	preach	near
team	cream	cheat	tease	tear
peace	scream	dream	bleach	clear

Can we eat cream on the beach by the sea?

Mom will teach Bea and Jean to read.

Each man on the team will sit on his seat.

I fear the beast will squeal for lean meat.

Dean will leave his desk clean and neat.

Sal sold sea shells at the sea shore.

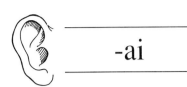

-ai

rain	air	aim	sail	chair
train	hair	claim	tail	chain
plain	fair	aid	nail	wait
brain	flair	paid	snail	jail
grain	gain	pain	mail	raid
stain	Spain	paint	saint	braid

Gail is running to the fair in the rain.

Craig will claim that he paid the bill.

Can Blair stain or paint the chair?

The rain in Spain lands on the plain.

I am afraid that Gail is in pain again.  again

I have faith that the Lord will save me.

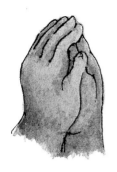

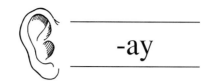

-ay

day	lay	ray	say	tray
way	pay	gray	slay	sway
hay	play	pray	bay	stay
may	clay	spray	bray	jay
bay	stay	stray	Kay	Fay

you	come	again	some	other

Kay will not stray from the yard.

Can you stay and play with me?

Fay will pray to the Lord to help her.

Ray will pay for hay for the horse.

Help Faith find the way to the bay to swim.

Rain, rain, go away; come again some other day.

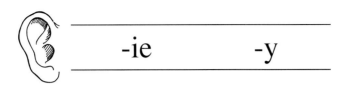
-ie   -y

pie	pies	by	cry	cries
tie	ties	my	fry	fries
lie	tries	dry	fly	flies
die	lies	sky	try	tries
vie	dies	shy	why	dries

I will try to fly my kite up in the sky.

I can fry my chicken on the stove.

Pete said, "Let's eat beef and fries!"

Will the babe cry when she lies in her crib?

Can Sis dry her shirt and skirt in the sun?

Why are the flies trying to eat Jane's pie?

If at first you fail, try, try again.

-oa

boat	toast	loan	goal	soap
coat	roast	foam	coal	soak
goat	boast	groan	shoal	road
gloat	coast	board	moat	load
cloak	roach	toad	float	oak
oath	coach	oats	bloat	throat

I need soap to soak the spot off my coat.

See the sailboat floating in the bay.

I like roast beef, a bun, and milk.

Joan will get a loan at the bank.

I hope the roach will not find the toast!

The goat is roaming by the coast.

I see the toad on the road by the oak tree.

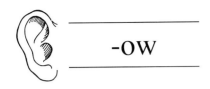 -ow

low	row	mow	show	flow
blow	grow	snow	bow	throw
crow	glow	slow	bowl	grown
elbow	widow	pillow	follow	shadow
below	window	yellow	fellow	morrow

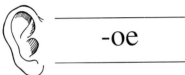 -oe

toe	go	foe	Joe	hoe
toes	goes	woe	Joe's	hoes

Can you see the crow on the snow by the window?

Did Joe cut his toe or his elbow with the hoe?

Let me tie the yellow bow on the pillow.

Show me stars that glow in the sky.

Joan will row the boat down the stream.

-ee	-ea	-ai	-ay
meet	eat	pain	ray
street	sea	rain	pray
screen	seal	sprain	spray
screech	pea	maid	stray
three	plea	stain	X-ray
bleed	flea	chain	today

-ie	-oa	-ow	-oe
lied	road	rainbow	doe
spied	roach	shadow	oboe
shied	loaf	follow	tip-toe
fried	coach	borrow	foe
tied	throat	widow	woe
untied	goat	elbow	roe

do	no	you	my	I	your
to	go	me	do	eye	don't

82

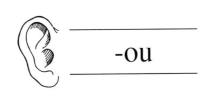

mouse	count	mouth	scout	our
house	couch	south	trout	out
loud	sound	found	spout	bout
cloud	pound	bound	sound	spout
noun	proud	pouch	ground	blouse

The scouts want to fish for trout in the stream.

They will camp on the ground under the clouds.

She found a mouse in the house by the couch.

Brad and Greg will play outside our house.

Get a pound of ground round at the store.

The spout on our teapot made a loud sound.

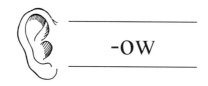
-ow

cow	down	owl	clown	tower
how	town	fowl	gown	bower
now	frown	plow	howl	power
brown	powder	crowd	jowl	flower
drown	chowder	crown	growl	shower

How now, brown cow!

Let's have a pow-wow in the tower.

We can go down town and get the chowder.

The five vowels are: a, e, i, o, u.

Jack and Jill went up the hill
    To fetch a pail of water;
Jack fell down and broke his crown,
    And Jill came tumbling after.

water

ce	ci	cy		
se	si	sy		

sent	sell	site	sea	sit
cent	cell	cite	cease	city
ace	ice	since	fence	peace
face	mice	mince	hence	fleece
pace	nice	quince	whence	brace
space	rice	wince	thence	pence
lace	price	prince	dunce	truce
place	lice	prance	dice	Bruce
race	slice	chance	spice	spruce
Grace	twice	dance	cinch	office
trace	thrice	France	Cindy	

Do you have a smile on your face?

Bruce said, "There is no place like home."

The Lord said, "Peace be with you."

ce   ci   cy

 palace   bicycle

 do   you   want   here

Do they sell ice cream cones here?

The price of a cone is ten cents.

Let's have a race to the white fence.

Bruce, come and race with me.

Here is the place for the spruce tree.

Do you want to eat my rice?

Three blind mice, see how they run!

Princess Grace lived in a palace far away.

Dennis said, "I want a green bicycle."

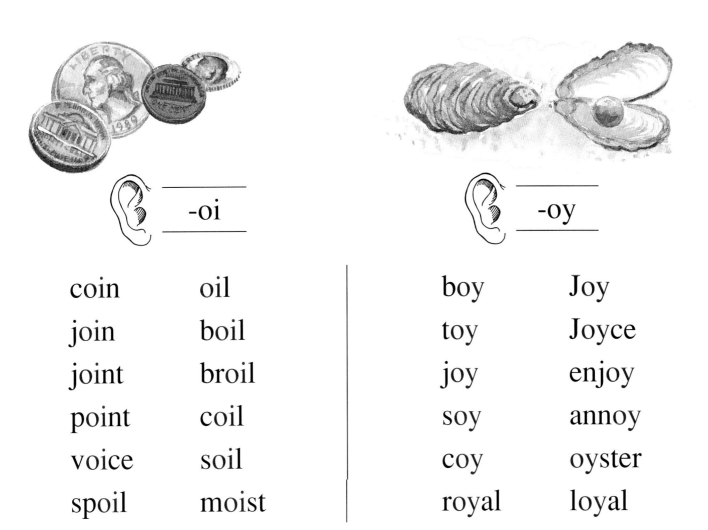

-oi		-oy	
coin	oil	boy	Joy
join	boil	toy	Joyce
joint	broil	joy	enjoy
point	coil	soy	annoy
voice	soil	coy	oyster
spoil	moist	royal	loyal

Joan said, "Joyce, come and join us."

What is your choice: to boil or broil the fish?

Roy hopes to go to West Point.

Joy enjoys playing with her toys.

The boy is loyal to his Dad.

The pig said, "Oink, oink."

 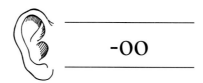 

moon	zoo	pool	cool	broom
soon	too	stool	fool	spoon
room	tooth	scoot	tool	loop
boom	food	bloom	spool	troop
noon	scoop	groom	stool	stoop

shampoo	balloon	afternoon	smooth
toadstool	baboon	rooster	teaspoon

 -oo

book	hook	good	wood	foot
cook	nook	hood	wool	soot
look	took	stood	room	hoof
crook	brook	shook	poor	cookie

looking	wooden	cooker	goodness woolen

At the zoo, we can see a moose, a goose,
    and a great big kangaroo.

The moon will not shine for us at noon.

Soon Barb's tooth will come out.

I want to swim in the pool in the afternoon.

Who said, "moo, moo" — the cow or the rooster?

Jean has a book on Winnie the Pooh and Piglet.

Brook will put boots on his feet.

Who will dress up like Little Red Riding Hood?

Dean will take his books to his room at home.

Here is proof that Joyce was a good cook.

The troops were marching into the woods.

The Goose and the Golden Eggs

A man found a wonderful goose on the road and took her home with him. Each day, she laid an egg made of gold. The gold eggs made the man very rich.

But the more gold eggs he got, the more gold the man wanted.

The man made up his mind to get all the golden eggs the goose had inside her. So he killed the goose and cut her open.

But the goose did not have lots of gold eggs inside her. She was just like any other goose inside.

Since the goose had been cut open, she could not lay any more golden eggs.

Don't be greedy. You may lose what you already have.

Aesop

90

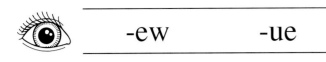

	-ew		-ue	
crew	grew	blew	due	blue
screw	drew	brew	cue	glue
flew	Andrew	threw	clue	flue

-ew

new	dew	chew	stew	fewer
news	hew	chewy	spew	sewer
pew	few	newt	Lew	skewer

Sue has a blue jewel in her ring.

Lew flew in a plane to see us here.

That was good news for Andrew.

Drew was looking for his books.

Stew, chew your food well.

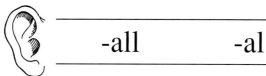 -all   -al

all	call	fall	salt	talk
ball	wall	mall	halt	walk
tall	hall	small	bald	balk
stall	gall	almost	scald	chalk
stalling	calling	falling	false	stalk

Do you like baseball, football, or
basketball better?

Jane can throw the ball almost to the wall.

Let's go to the mall to get a malt.

The horse was standing tall in his stall.

Pete and Fritz were crawling down the hall.

The Swing

How do you like to go up in a swing,
   Up in the air so blue?

Oh, I do think it the pleasantest thing
   Ever a child can do!

Up in the air and over the wall,
   Till I can see so wide,

Rivers and trees and cattle and all
   Over the countryside —

Till I look down on the garden green,
   Down on the roof so brown —

Up in the air I go flying again,
   Up in the air and down!

Robert Louis Stevenson, 1885

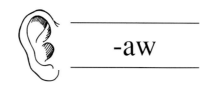
-aw

paw	saw	awe	bawl	dawn
raw	slaw	yawn	crawl	lawn
claw	law	hawk	shawl	draw
pawn	lawn	squawk	Shawn	drawn

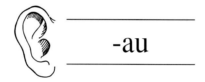
-au

haul	laud	fault	taut	daunt
maul	daub	vault	taunt	flaunt
Paul	Maud	sauce	haunt	gauze

Shawn will blow up a blue balloon.

I saw Paul haul the fawn with the hurt hoof.

It is the law to trim the lawn.

The hawk in the tree made a large squawk.

It's not Maud's fault that the chowder is cold.

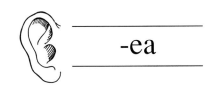 

-ea

red	rest	dead	breath	thread
read	breast	head	health	threat
bread	sweat	deaf	wealth	instead

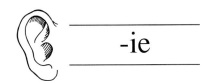

-ie

chief	piece	field	tier
brief	niece	shield	pier
grief	grieve	yield	pierce
thief	priest	wield	fierce
shriek	fief	belief	relief

The red hen flew away with her bread.

The feather was blowing in the wind.

Heather took a deep breath and shrieked.

The chief rode on a leather saddle.

The old flag said, "Don't tread on me."

The Little Red Hen

A Mouse, a Frog, and a Little Red Hen,
　　Together kept a house.
The Frog was very lazy,
　　And lazier still was the Mouse.

The work all fell on the Little Red Hen,
　　Who had to get the wood,
And make the fires, and scrub, and cook,
　　And sometimes hunt for food.

One day, as she was hopping around,
　　She found a bag of rye.
She said, "Who'll help me make some bread?"
　　Said the lazy Mouse, "Not I."

She asked the Frog as he lay in the shade,
　　But he also said, "Not I."
So the Hen worked hard with bowl and spoon,
　　And mixed and stirred the rye.

"Who'll make the fire to bake the bread?"
　　Said the Hen. But Mouse said, "Not I."
She asked the Frog to help her, please,
　　But Frog said again, "Not I."

The Little Red Hen kept working hard.
　　A roaring fire she made,
And while the bread was baking brown,
　　"Who'll set the table?" she said.

"Not I," said the sleepy Frog with a yawn.
　　"Not I," said the Mouse again.
So Hen set the table all by herself.
　　"Who'll eat this bread?" said the Hen.

"I will," said the Frog. "Me, too," squeaked
　　　the Mouse,
　　As they near the table drew.
"Oh, no, you won't!" said the Little Red Hen,
　　And away with the bread she flew.

My Shadow

I have a little shadow
  that goes in and out with me,

And what can be the use of him
  is more than I can see.

He is very, very like me
  from the heels up to the head;

And I see him jump before me,
  when I jump into my bed.

The funniest thing about him
  is the way he likes to grow —

Not at all like proper children,
  which is always very slow.

For he sometimes shoots up taller
  like an India-rubber ball,

And he sometimes gets so little
  that there's none of him at all.

Robert Louis Stevenson, 1885

The Rabbit and the Turtle

The rabbit was always boasting about how fast he can run. He made fun of the turtle because he was so slow.

One day, the turtle said, "I am tired of your sneers. Let's have a race, and I know I can beat you." "That's nonsense," said the rabbit. "You can't do it!"

The turtle said, "I think I can beat you. We can race down the road to the big rock by the pond."

Soon the rabbit was far ahead of the turtle, who crawled along the road slowly. The rabbit said to himself, "This race is a big joke. I have time to take a little nap in the grass and still win after I wake up."

Meanwhile, the turtle kept on crawling. He did not give up. He passed the sleeping rabbit. When the rabbit woke up, the turtle had already reached the big rock.

The one who keeps going will win the race.

Aesop

The Wind and the Leaves

"Come, little leaves," said the wind one day.
"Come over the meadows with me, and play;
Put on your dresses of red and gold,
Summer is gone, and the days grow cold."

Soon as the leaves heard the wind's loud call,
Down they came fluttering, one and all;
Over the brown fields they danced and flew,
Singing the soft little songs they knew.

Dancing and whirling the little leaves went;
Winter had called them and they were content.
Soon fast asleep in their earthy beds,
The snow laid a coverlet over their heads.

George Cooper

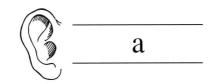

a

way	like	bout	side	lone
away	alike	about	aside	alone

wake	live	cute	rise	mass
awake	alive	acute	arise	amass

sleep	do	maze	glow	mend
asleep	ado	amaze	aglow	amend

head	float	foot	jar	miss
ahead	afloat	afoot	ajar	amiss

pace	fair	muse	side	fire
apace	affair	amuse	aside	afire

part	while	woke	blaze	drift
apart	awhile	awoke	ablaze	adrift

Grace is afraid Joan is still asleep.

But she awoke and came out to amuse us.

Alice	always	acorn	apron

_____
wh
_____

 when   whip   which   whim

 who   what   where   why

| wish | win | eye | do | were |
| which | whim | why | who | where |

Whether the weather be fine,

Or whether the weather be not,

Whether the weather be cold,

Or whether the weather be hot,

We'll weather the weather

Whatever the weather,

Whether we like it or not!

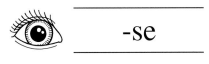 -se

z

rose	rise	as	noise
nose	wise	cause	raise
dose	arise	because	praise
hose	ease	pause	these
close	please	clause	those
chose	tease	applause	suppose
choose	seas	reason	Rose

"Please" and "thank you" are sweet words.

The applause for the singing made a loud noise.

Ros will arise each morning and praise the Lord.

You can choose these roses or those daisies.

I try hard because I want to read my book.

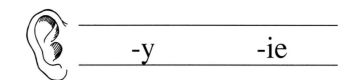

-y   -ie

bell	bud	chunk	dirt	goof
belly	buddy	chunky	dirty	goofy
jell	bug	cock	fish	pony
jelly	buggy	cocky	fishy	ponies
jiff	mist	part	rock	sauce
jiffy	misty	party	Rocky	saucy
Bill	Jim	Dad	Bob	Sam
Billy	Jimmy	Daddy	Bobby	Sammy
kitty	daddy	penny	city	body
kitties	daddies	pennies	cities	bodies
party	baby	funny	army	cookie
parties	babies	funnies	armies	cookies
carry	bunny	forty	fifty	candy
carries	bunnies	forties	fifties	candies

The Fox and the Crow

A crow stole a big piece of cheese from a farm window and carried it up in a tall tree.

A fox saw this happen and said to himself, "If I am smart, I can have cheese for my supper." So the foxy fox made a plan.

"Good morning, Miss Crow," he said. "How beautiful you look today. Your feathers shine in the sun. Your neck is as graceful as a swan's, and your wings are strong like an eagle's. I bet you can sing as sweetly as a nightingale."

The crow was so pleased with such praise that she wanted to prove she had a sweet voice.

When she opened her mouth to say "Caw, Caw," the cheese fell to the ground and the fox snapped it up.

Don't be fooled by a lot of praise.

Aesop

| 20 | 30 | 40 | 50 | 60 | 70 |

I can count: ten, twenty, thirty, forty, fifty,

sixty, seventy.

Kelly calls her funny dolls Amy and Lucy.

Sally will carry a kitty and a bunny to the party.

Harry will amuse the ladies at the tea party.

Katie prays to the Lord daily.

Don't be silly; Connie is not angry.

Jackie took Tony to see the Smoky Mountains.

Debbie will bring daisies home in the car.

Did Nancy empty the pennies from your pocket?

Is Billy too heavy to ride on the pony?

It is too chilly to be cozy in the buggy.

I like little kitty, her fur is so warm;

And if I don't hurt her, she'll do me no harm.

I'll not pull her tail, nor drive her away,

But kitty and I very gently will play.

She will sit by my side,
    and I'll give her some food;

And she'll love me because
    I am gentle and good.

Good, better, best,

Never let it rest,

Till your good is better,

And your better is best.

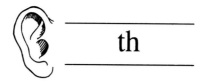

th

rash	rush	rill	rob	rice
thrash	thrush	thrill	throb	thrice
rust	row	rift	grew	goat
thrust	throw	thrift	threw	throat
bone	drive	ball	bread	Brett
throne	thrive	thrall	thread	threat

sc	sp	st

ape	lit	rung	ring	rang
scrape	split	sprung	string	sprang
raw	truck	read	rig	crew
straw	struck	spread	sprig	screw
rank	rout	ramble	crunch	rub
shrank	sprout	scramble	scrunch	scrub

| -ge | -dge | -age | 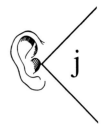 j

age	huge	urge	bandage
cage	lunge	surge	cabbage
page	plunge	purge	sausage
wage	binge	splurge	village

sage	cringe	large	garbage
rage	hinge	charge	package
stage	fringe	singe	postage

| badge | fudge | ridge | edge |
| cadge | judge | bridge | ledge |

Madge	budge	dodge	pledge
grudge	nudge	lodge	sledge
trudge	smudge	wedge	fledge

-ge   -dge j

Madge has the urge to play dodge ball.

I made a hodge-podge of sausage and cabbage.

Bridget will make a large pan of fudge.

Please don't get a smudge on my page.

George is in charge of the badges.

London Bridge is falling down.

 to   two   too

Rick gave a ball to Dave.

Rick gave two balls to Zack.

Rick gave two balls to Kate, too.

yes	here	now	up	come	in
no	there	then	down	go	out

The Ant and the Grasshopper

One day in the late summer, an ant was busy finding some grains and hiding them to eat during the long winter.

A grasshopper hopped by and said, "Don't work so hard. Come and dance with me in the falling leaves." The ant said, "I have no time to play. I must get ready for winter." So the grasshopper hopped away.

When winter came, there was no food on the ground and the grasshopper was hungry. He said to the ant, "Please give me some of your grain so I won't starve."

But the ant said, "You wasted your time singing and dancing when the weather was warm. Now you have to pay the price for being so foolish."

It's smart to prepare today for the needs of tomorrow.

Aesop

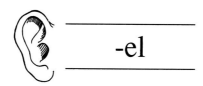 -el

barrel	damsel	hostel	nickel
cancel	easel	jewel	morsel
vessel	flannel	kernel	channel
parcel	Hazel	marvel	model
pretzel	quarrel	scalpel	tassel

 -le  -el

turtle	battle	cattle	rattle
little	beetle	uncle	ripple
puzzle	bugle	tickle	gentle
ankle	eagle	cradle	jungle
wiggle	maple	meddle	candle
wrestle	jingle	struggle	fumble

_____ -or 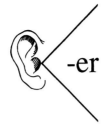 -er

doctor	honor	author	mirror
minor	sailor	color	victor
favor	razor	motor	sponsor
flavor	labor	tenor	parlor
suitor	humor	candor	rumor

The doctor will treat Jim's ankle.

The baby in the cradle has a rattle.

It takes a lot of labor to be a good singer.

Nick blew the bugle to call the sailors.

"Mirror, mirror on the wall,

who's the fairest of us all?"

The Dog and His Bone

A dog stole a large bone and was carrying it back to his home. When he crossed a bridge, he looked down and the pond acted like a mirror.

The dog said to himself, "I see another dog in the pond with a bigger bone in his mouth than I have."

Then the dog said, "I want that other dog's bone, too." So he snarled and grabbed for the other bone he saw in the pond.

As soon as the dog opened his mouth, his own bone fell to the bottom of the pond.

Then, the dog didn't have any bone at all.

Don't grab for something that is not your own.

Aesop

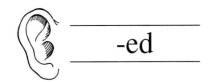 -ed

| taste | print | toast | weed |
| tasted | printed | toasted | weeded |

| paste | crowd | rest | mend |
| pasted | crowded | rested | mended |

| blend | cart | count | dust |
| blended | carted | counted | dusted |

| test | shout | seat | shade |
| tested | shouted | seated | shaded |

| heat | mend | treat | braid |
| heated | mended | treated | braided |

| plant | float | need | boast |
| planted | floated | needed | boasted |

| hunt | wade | point | crowd |
| hunted | waded | pointed | crowded |

| sound | start | fold | lift |
| sounded | started | folded | lifted |

115

Connie waded too far in the sea and started to cry.

She shouted for help and Dad lifted her up.

Paul counted twenty boys at the crowded beach.

Bridget boasted that she made a boat that floated.

ended	landed	wicked	coasted
spotted	handed	blasted	jagged
branded	nodded	wooded	skated
hoisted	reported	shredded	blessed

There was a crooked man,
    And he walked a crooked mile,
He found a crooked sixpence
    Against a crooked stile;
He bought a crooked cat,
    Which caught a crooked mouse,
And they all lived together
    In a little crooked house.

-ed   **-d**

rain	sail	fill	curl
rained	sailed	filled	curled
plan	turn	pin	boil
planned	turned	pinned	boiled
can	skin	please	wheel
canned	skinned	pleased	wheeled
call	wing	pray	trail
called	winged	prayed	trailed
play	kill	squeeze	brag
played	killed	squeezed	bragged
flag	roll	breathe	will
flagged	rolled	breathed	willed
turn	sail	slam	charm
turned	sailed	slammed	charmed
buzz	drag	follow	fan
buzzed	dragged	followed	fanned

Mom braided Jane's brown hair.

I dreamed I got a two-wheeled bicycle.

We are going to see the doctor about my hand.

Come and sing "The Star Spangled Banner."

Some boys played the bugle and the horn.

Tony was burned when he squeezed the pot.

Jack skinned his knee when he sailed his boat.

Jane dressed up and curled her hair for a party.

Charles and Fritz were planning to camp out.

Madge filled some bowls with milk.

Then, she put them out for the kitty to drink.

Blair shouted when Luke sailed our boat.

-ed		-t	
stop	flush	kiss	tap
stopped	flushed	kissed	tapped
cash	puff	kick	box
cashed	puffed	kicked	boxed
hatch	stuff	wish	smoke
hatched	stuffed	wished	smoked
latch	fuss	fish	fix
latched	fussed	fished	fixed
crack	bake	mix	like
cracked	baked	mixed	liked
back	race	skip	slice
backed	raced	skipped	sliced
wax	trace	miss	price
waxed	traced	missed	priced
flash	pace	pitch	smash
flashed	paced	pitched	smashed

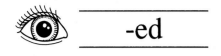 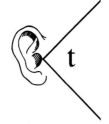 

-ed   t

peck	reach	poach	march
pecked	reached	poached	marched
wreck	preach	hitch	mark
wrecked	preached	hitched	marked
stretch	bleach	fetch	vex
stretched	bleached	fetched	vexed
jerk	splash	sniff	wink
jerked	splashed	sniffed	winked
back	milk	mix	cap
backed	milked	mixed	capped

Who huffed and puffed to blow

    the pig's house down?

I wished that Mom had baked a cake.

Rich kicked the ball and it smashed in the wall.

We gassed up the car and raced into town.

mother	mama	son	sister
father	papa	daughter	brother
now	was	were	great

Reed pitched the baseball left-handed.

Bert fished and hunted in the woods.

Gail counted some eggs and then poached them.

Then she sliced some bread and toasted it.

We were all seated when the horses raced.

We were going to see our uncle, but it rained.

Our car stopped when the great storm started.

Mom rested while Nancy cooked the beans.

I was inside, but Sue and Paul were outside.

Our Father and Mother played ball with us.

Our sister's name is Sally.

Our brother's name is Luke.

rabbit	tomcat	cowboy
earthquake	helmet	heaven
pumpkin	boxtop	chapter
peanut	visit	master
kidnap	turkey	shelter
hotdog	harvest	finish
ticket	puppet	rocket
napkin	husband	capsule
trumpet	tablet	kitchen
absent	baseball	beaver
gallon	football	member
dragon	soccer	pilgrim
inside	hockey	saucer
spider	almost	honest
sweater	surprise	raccoon
dozen	golden	rubber
nickel	children	plenty
quarter	slippers	behave
dollar	packet	shadow
milkmaid	nonsense	hundred

The Milkmaid and Her Milk

A milkmaid was carrying a bucket of milk to market on her head without using her hands. As she went down the road, she said to herself:

"I shall sell this milk for a good price and use the money to buy three dozen eggs. Then, I shall put the eggs under our old hen and soon I will have a yard full of chickens.

"Then, I shall sell the chickens and buy a new dress with a matching jacket and a hat with ribbons. When I go to the fair in my new dress, all the boys will dance with me and all the girls will wish they had a dress like mine. I'll be so proud and I'll toss my head like this!"

So she tossed her head! That knocked the bucket off her head, and the milk spilled all over the road.

Don't count your chickens before they are hatched.

Aesop

123

railroad	outside	birthday
cricket	iceskate	morning
number	password	bedtime
pretend	mailman	splendid
goblin	spaceship	hungry
harbor	grateful	lifeboat
between	question	battle
apple	punish	flashlight
report	chopstick	sailboat
suppose	over	monkey
chapel	sandwich	splendid
sometimes	contest	seven
airplane	dentist	summer
rescue	haircut	winter
ribbon	eyeball	sister
padlock	funny	hunter
tunnel	dustpan	rooster
yellow	burger	chicken
purple	milkshake	teacher
safety	better	monster

The Cat and the Mice

The mice were afraid of the cat. So, the mice held a meeting to decide how to save themselves from the cat.

One mouse had a good plan. He said, "We can tie a little bell around the cat's neck. It will tinkle every time the cat moves. The bell will warn us, and we can all run to safety."

All the mice said this was a splendid plan.

But then one mouse said, "Which mouse will hang the bell on the cat?"

All the mice were afraid to do that. They did not want to go near the cat.

It's easy to think up a plan, but it is harder to carry it out.

Aesop

cabin	under	steamship
mermaid	never	missile
secret	toothbrush	Sunday
after	hairbrush	Monday
paper	whisper	Thursday
pencil	traffic	Friday
spider	shiver	package
treatment	circle	twenty
tiger	circus	thirty
bracelet	became	forty
northwest	downstairs	fifty
beaver	upstairs	sixty
footprint	bedroom	ninety
cockroach	picnic	southwest
closet	because	mustard
warehouse	until	broken
weather	April	rainbow
windshield	August	Easter
breakfast	catfish	snowflake
city	tennis	dashboard
country	streetcar	button
blanket	drummer	stronger

The Wind and the Sun

The wind and the sun were boasting about who was stronger. "I am the strongest power in the world," said the sun. "No,"said the wind, "I am stronger than you are."

"Let's find out," said the sun. "Do you see that man walking down the road? Let's see which one of us can make him take off his coat faster." "O.K.," said the wind. "I'll try first."

The sun hid behind a cloud while the wind blew very hard. The man shivered. The wind roared and sent cold blasts against the man. The harder the wind blew, the more the man wrapped his coat around him.

"Now it's my turn," said the sun, as it came out from behind the cloud. The shining sun made the man warm. First, he unbuttoned his coat. The sun kept sending its warm rays down to earth. Soon, the man got hot and took off his coat.

"I won the contest!" said the sun.

It's better to be warm and gentle than cold and mean.

Aesop

127

Sarah	Morgan	Michael	Jeffrey
Ashley	Kathleen	Matthew	Allen
Megan	Sophie	Nathan	Richard
Michelle	Anna	Steven	Barney
Lauren	Jenny	David	Patrick
Christine	Holly	Daniel	Brendan
Rachel	Janet	Tyler	Martin
Lindsey	Casey	Justin	Austin
Shannon	Shelley	Brian	Kenneth
Whitney	Lisa	Robert	Oscar
Kelsey	Vincent	Jacob	Bradley
Mary	Walter	Robin	Calvin
Christy	Dennis	Andrew	Peter
Amber	Roger	Jason	Wesley
Laura	Travis	Mitchell	Raymond
Noel	Kevin	Adam	Douglas
Julie	William	Lucas	Spencer
Linda	Derek	Alex	Henry

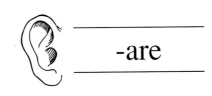 

-are

bare	hare	mare	aware
dare	pare	stare	declare
care	snare	flare	prepare
fare	spare	blare	parent

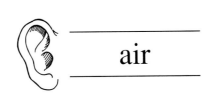 

air

air	chair	affair	airy
hair	flair	impair	dairy
fair	stair	eclair	fairy
pair	lair	solitaire	hairy

I'm glad we had a spare tire when we had a flat.

Here are a pair of chairs for the twins.

A hare is a rabbit. A mare is a horse.

129

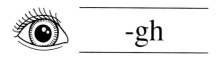 -gh

high	sight	light	fight	caught
sigh	tight	flight	fright	taught
thigh	might	plight	upright	daughter
nigh	right	slight	tonight	slaughter
night	bright	blight	delight	naughty
		straight		

It is night, so we must turn on the light.

Almighty God tells us always to be upright.

Tony got in a fight, so he had to take flight.

George hurt his thigh in the fight.

It is hard to draw a straight line.

Mother taught her daughter to read.

The Lion and the Mouse

One day a mouse ran over the paws of a sleeping lion. The lion woke up and was angry. He was about to crush the little animal when the mouse cried, "Please, mighty lion, spare me. I am such a tiny mouthful. If you let me go, some day I might be able to help you."

The idea of the little mouse helping the powerful beast amused the lion so much that he let him go.

Some time later, the lion got caught in a hunter's net. The more he struggled to get loose, the tighter the net held him. He roared with rage.

Hearing the lion, the mouse ran to the trap and began to bite the net. Soon he had chewed the ropes loose and set the huge lion free.

Little things may some day be very important.

Aesop

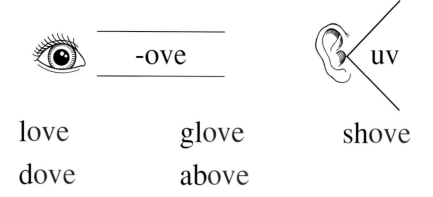

love   glove   shove

dove   above

Evening

God is by me when I pray.
    And when I close my eyes at night,
I know that He will with me stay,
    When others are all out of sight.

For He who rules the stars and sea,
    Who makes the grass and trees to grow,
Will bless a little child like me,
    When on my knees my love I show.

He holds all things in His right hand,
    The rich, the poor, the great, the small.
When we sleep, or sit, or stand,
    We know that God still loves us all.

Thomas Miller, 1850

Hey diddle, diddle,
The cat and the fiddle,
The cow jumped over the moon;
The little dog laughed
To see such sport,
And the dish ran away with the spoon.

-on   un   wun

son   money   come   one
done   honey   some   once

133

1	one	6	six
2	two	7	seven
3	three	8	eight
4	four	9	nine
5	five	10	ten

One, two, buckle my shoe,
Three, four, shut the door,
Five, six, pick up sticks,
Seven, eight, lay them straight.
Nine, ten, a big fat hen.

b	k	t	w

b	k	t	w
lamb	knot	listen	wrap
jamb	knob	often	wrist
comb	knap	soften	write
climb	knee	fasten	writer
numb	kneel	castle	wrote
debt	knelt	nestle	wrest
limb	knell	bustle	wren
dumb	knife	rustle	wrench
crumb	knit	hustle	wreck
thumb	knock	bristle	wring
plumber	knick	glisten	wrong
doubt	knack	moisten	wretch
bomb	knead	hasten	wrung
bombing	knuckle	whistle	wreath
comb	know	thistle	written
combing	knight	epistle	wrestle

A flashlight will shine brightly at night.

I might see Thomas tonight in the castle.

John cut the knot on his knapsack with a knife.

The plumber came to fasten the faucet.

Sarah has bandages on her knee and wrist.

build	John	talk
guess	Thomas	walk
guest	Esther	balk
guitar	honest	half
guide	hour	calf
guard	rhino	halves
guinea pig	spaghetti	calves

All You Do

When the stars, at set of sun,
Watch you from on high;
When the morning light has come,
Know the Lord is nigh.

All you do, and all you say,
He can see and hear;
When you work and when you play,
Know the Lord is near.

All your joys and griefs He knows,
Sees each smile and tear;
When to him you tell your woes,
Know the Lord will hear.

The Donkey in the Lion's Skin

A donkey once found the skin of a dead lion. The donkey wrapped himself in the lion's skin like a coat and strutted around the woods. He said to himself, "Now I am dressed like a lion! So I can be king of the jungle!"

All the other animals were scared except the fox, who said, "Something is wrong with that lion."

The donkey said to himself, "I will roar and that will frighten the fox." But when the donkey opened his mouth, he didn't roar like a lion. He brayed like a donkey.

The fox laughed and said, "I might have been afraid if you had kept your mouth shut."

Clothes do not make the man. What comes out of your mouth tells what you really are.

Aesop

Little Things

Little drops of water,
    Little grains of sand,
Make the mighty ocean
    And the beautiful land.

And the little moments,
    Humble though they be,
Make the mighty ages
    Of eternity.

So our little errors
    Lead the soul away,
From the path of virtue
    Into sin to stray.

Little deeds of kindness,
    Little words of love,
Make our earth a Paradise,
    Like the Heaven above.

Julia A. Carney, 1855

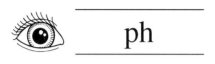 ph  f

phone	elephant	phase	phonics
telephone	dolphin	phrase	Philip
graph	nephew	phantom	Phyllis
telegraph	orphan	prophet	Ralph
photograph	microphone	gopher	Joseph

Joseph will take a photograph of his nephew.

The prophets in the Old Testament were wise men.

Let's go to the zoo and see elephants and dolphins.

I will call Phyllis on the telephone.

The Eagle and the Turtle

A turtle was moaning and groaning about his life. "I'm tired of just crawling on the ground," he said, "I want to fly and glide in the air."

He asked the eagle to help him try to fly. But the eagle warned him, "Your body is not built for flying."

"Yes, I can fly," said the turtle. "I've watched how the birds do it. I can make my four flippers flap like wings. Please carry me up high and I will show you I can fly."

So the eagle carried the turtle up high and said, "Now, see what you can do." But as soon as the eagle let go, the turtle fell straight down like a rock and was smashed in little pieces.

Don't try to be somebody you are not.

Aesop

_____ -ou

 -oe -oo -u -aw

| -o | -oo | -oo | -u | -aw |
doe	moon	book	cuff	paw
dough	you	could	rough	ought
though	your	couldn't	tough	sought
although	soup	would	enough	fought
shoulder	through	wouldn't	young	bought
furlough	group	should	touch	brought
	Lou	shouldn't		thought
				fourth

 _____ gh    f

laugh	rough	cough
laughter	tough	trough
laughing		

142

Happy Thought

The world is so full of a number of things,
I'm sure we should all be as happy as kings.

Robert Louis Stevenson, 1885

I had a little pig,
I put him in the trough.
I fed him so much
That his tail popped off!

Work while you work,
Play while you play.
One thing at a time,
That is the way.

All that you do,
Do with your might.
Things done by halves,
Are not done right.

The Boy and the Wolf

One day a boy, who was hired to look after the sheep, thought he would have some fun. So he rushed to the village crying "Wolf! Wolf!" The grown-ups came running with clubs and pitchforks to chase away the wolf.

But there was no wolf! The boy laughed at his joke, but the adults did not laugh.

The next week, the boy cried "Wolf! Wolf!" again. Again the people came to help him save the sheep. And again they found that the boy had tricked them.

One day, a wolf really came out of the woods. But when the boy cried "Wolf! Wolf!" nobody came to help. So the wolf enjoyed a good meal of sheep and lamb.

A liar will not be believed even when he tells the truth.

Aesop

144

Mary Had a Little Lamb

Mary had a little lamb,
    Its fleece was white as snow;
And everywhere that Mary went
    The lamb was sure to go.

It followed her to school one day.
    That was against the rule.
It made the children laugh and play
    To see a lamb at school.

"Why does the lamb love Mary so?"
    The eager children cry.
"Why Mary loves the lamb, you know,"
    The teacher did reply.

The Star

Twinkle, twinkle, little star,
    How I wonder what you are!
Up above the world so high,
    Like a diamond in the sky.

When the blazing sun is gone,
    When it nothing shines upon,
Then you show your little light,
    Twinkle, twinkle, all the night.

In the dark blue sky you keep,
    And often through my curtains peep,
For you never shut your eye,
    Till the sun is in the sky.

As your bright and tiny spark,
    Lights the traveler in the dark,
Though I know not what you are,
    Twinkle, twinkle, little star.

Jane Taylor, 1806

All Things Bright and Beautiful

All things bright and beautiful,
    All creatures great and small,
All things wise and wonderful,
    The Lord God made them all.

Each little flower that opens,
    Each little bird that sings,
He made their glowing colors,
    He made their tiny wings.

The purple-headed mountain,
    The river running by,
The sunset, and the morning
    That brightens up the sky;

The cold wind in the winter,
    The pleasant summer sun,
The ripe fruits in the garden,
    He made them every one.

He gave us eyes to see them,
    And lips that we might tell,
How great is God Almighty,
    Who made all things so well.

Cecil Frances Alexander, 1848

Jack Sprat could eat no fat,
   His wife could eat no lean.
And so, between the two of them,
   They licked the platter clean.

Humpty Dumpty sat on a wall,
Humpty Dumpty had a great fall.
All the king's horses
   and all the king's men,
Couldn't put Humpty
   together again.

Whole Duty of Children

A child should always say what's true
And speak when he is spoken to,
And behave mannerly at table;
At least as far as he is able.

Robert Louis Stevenson, 1885

Bed In Summer

In winter I get up at night
    And dress by yellow candle-light.
In summer, quite the other way,
    I have to go to bed by day.

I have to go to bed and see
    The birds still hopping on the tree,
Or hear the grown-up people's feet
    Still going past me in the street.

And does it not seem hard to you,
    When all the sky is clear and blue,
And I should like so much to play,
    To have to go to bed by day?

Robert Louis Stevenson, 1885

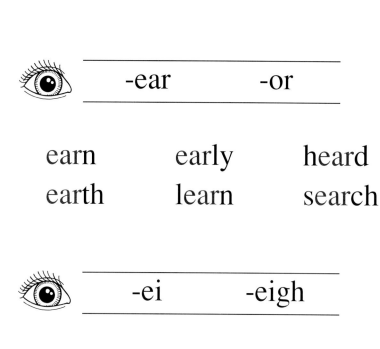

-ear   -or

| earn | early | heard | work | word |
| earth | learn | search | worm | worst |

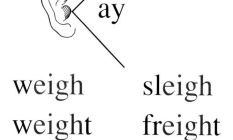 ur

-ei   -eigh

| vein | heir | eight | weigh | sleigh |
| reins | their | eighth | weight | freight |

ay

ch

| Christ | Christian | chorus | school |
| Christmas | character | chemist | Pinocchio |

 k

There was an old owl
   who lived in an oak;
The more he heard, the less he spoke.
The less he spoke, the more he heard.
Why aren't we like that wise old bird?

Time To Wake Up

A birdie with a yellow bill
Hopped upon my window sill,
Cocked his shining eye and said:
"Aren't you 'shamed, you sleepy-head?"

Robert Louis Stevenson, 1885

Cocks crow in the morn
To tell us to rise,
And if you sleep late,
You'll never be wise.
For early to bed
And early to rise
Makes a man healthy,
Wealthy and wise.

peppermint	ladybug	holiday
argument	yesterday	animal
hospital	submarine	valentine
testament	gunpowder	dangerous
conductor	happiness	suddenly
anywhere	celebrate	banana
porcupine	janitor	punishment
equipment	visitor	medicine
appetite	Columbus	eleven
electric	telephone	calendar
photograph	telegram	alphabet
vanilla	telegraph	potato
chocolate	telescope	hamburger
parachute	bicycle	seventeen
battleship	tricycle	residence
difficult	carpenter	grasshopper
passenger	location	disaster
family	imitate	camera
different	rollerskate	afternoon
wonderful	hurricane	liberty

Thirty days hath September,
April, June and November.
All the rest have thirty-one,
Excepting February alone,
Which has four and twenty-four
Till leap-year gives it one day more.

Little Jack Horner
Sat in the corner
Eating his Christmas pie.
He put in his thumb,
And pulled out a plum,
And said,
"What a good boy am I!"

Matthew, Mark, Luke and John,
Bless the bed that I lie on.
If I should die before I wake,
I pray the Lord my soul to take.

newspaper
octopus
buffalo
surrender
remember
invited
cultivate
department
furniture
accident
vaccinate
hesitate
minister
butterfly
clarinet
magazine
president
promotion
recognize
reflection
assistant
umbrella

policeman
refreshment
propeller
pretended
mistaken
instrument
excitement
excellent
grandmother
grandfather
enemies
candidate
seventy
pharmacy
collection
completely
concentrate
motorboat
possible
happiness
barbecue
astronaut

crocodile
elephant
strawberry
tomato
gingerbread
volleyball
basketball
vitamin
wastebasket
wheelbarrow
wilderness
chimpanzee
woodpecker
demonstrate
detective
kangaroo
domino
eyeglasses
gentleman
hide-and-seek
rattlesnake
appendix

Can you name all the ways we can go places?

We can go on a bicycle, a tricycle, or a scooter.
We might go on a motorcycle.
We can go in a car or an automobile or a van.
We might go in a truck or a jeep.
We might even ride on a horse or a pony.

We can go on a bus or streetcar.
We can go on a railroad train. Trains and
     subways have to stay on a track.
We can go in a motorboat or sailboat.

We can ride on an airplane. Some planes have
     jet engines, and some have propellers.
We might go in a helicopter.

We can walk or run or jog.

America has a great transportation system.
Which way do you like to ride?

Jessica	Zachary	Tiffany
Brittany	Nicholas	Jacqueline
Amanda	Jonathan	Marissa
Samantha	Christopher	Natalie
Jennifer	Benjamin	Alexis
Maria	Timothy	Andrea
Stephanie	Samuel	Gabrielle
Priscilla	Gregory	Valerie
Christina	Jeremy	Abigail
Rebecca	Oliver	Margaret
Caroline	Anthony	Patricia
Emily	Thaddeus	Alicia
Catherine	Juliet	Pamela
Allison	Rosalind	Annabel
Kimberly	Joshua	Elinor
Melissa	Atlanta	September
Saturday	Saint Louis	October
Thanksgiving	Baltimore	November
Halloween	Washington	December

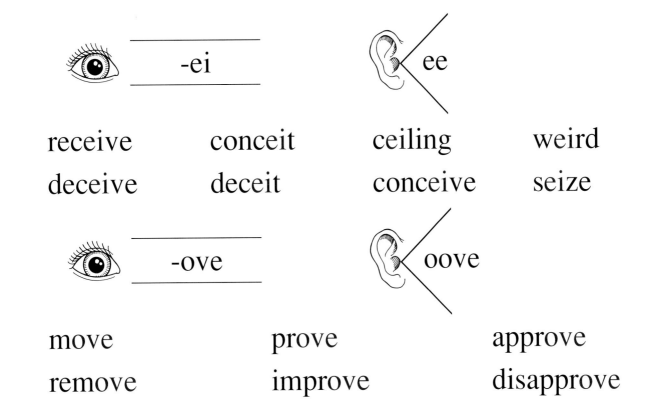

-ei

receive   conceit

deceive   deceit

ee

ceiling   weird

conceive   seize

-ove

move   prove   approve

remove   improve   disapprove

 wash   put   push   bush

It is weird to see the bush on the ceiling.

Let me prove that I can read.

I will wash myself every day.

I hope Mom and Dad approve of my work.

Let me guess where you put my book.

The Wind

Who has seen the wind?
    Neither I nor you;
But when the leaves hang trembling
    The wind is passing through.

Who has seen the wind?
    Neither you nor I;
But when the trees bow down their heads,
    The wind is passing by.

Christina Rossetti, 1872

How many weather disasters can you name?

snowstorm	tornado	cyclone
hailstorm	volcano	hurricane
sleetstorm	avalanche	monsoon
thunderstorm	blizzard	typhoon
lightning	earthquake	tidal wave

-tion   -sion   -cian   -tian    shun

nation	action	mansion	musician
ration	vacation	mission	physician
station	motion	pension	magician
notion	adoption	session	Dalmatian

plantation	starvation	foundation
transportation	celebration	occupation
education	vaccination	hesitation
carnation	confession	condition

We will meet Kathleen at the train station.

I have a notion she will be on vacation.

Allison wants to become a musician.

Let's have a celebration when we finish this book!

-sion  zhun

vision   television   conversion

fusion   conclusion   confusion

version   transfusion   collusion

 -sure  zher

treasure   closure   seizure

pleasure   enclosure   leisure

measure   azure

 -ture  cher

picture   rupture

capture   adventure

fracture   scripture

 -ous us

joyous   famous   tremendous

nervous   glorious   monstrous

Which One Loved Mother Best?

"I love you, Mother," said little Mike.
Forgetting his work, he rode off on his bike.
He joined his pals in the park for a swing,
Leaving his mother the groceries to bring.

"I love you, Mother," said Anabel.
"I love you and I think you're swell."
Then she teased and pouted half the day,
Till Mother was glad when she went out to play.

"I love you, Mother," said Mary Ann.
Today, I'll help you all I can.
She washed the dishes and got a broom,
She swept the floor and dusted the room.

"I love you Mother," again they said —
Three little children going to bed.
How do you think that Mother guessed
Which of them really loved her best?

Joy Allison

helicopter	caterpillar	January
celebration	transportation	February
conversation	knickerbocker	invitation
education	emergency	entertainment
communicate	anticipate	occupation
barracuda	macaroni	immediate
elevator	comfortable	Cinderella
supermarket	temperature	Olivia
citizenship	mathematics	Elizabeth
navigator	misunderstand	Victoria
vegetable	gladiator	Alexander
magnificent	television	Alexandra
roller coaster	altogether	San Francisco
alligator	calculator	New York City
kindergarten	escalator	America
automobile	arithmetic	United States
impossible	independence	Mississippi
combination	democracy	Colorado

The Eagle and the Chicken

Once upon a time, the eagle and the chicken were friends. They would fly over the countryside and hunt for food together.

One day, they flew over a farm and met a cow who was eating corn. The cow said, "Help yourself. The farmer gives us plenty to eat." This was a surprise to the eagle and the chicken, who always had to work hard to find their food. So they stuffed themselves with the free food.

The chicken liked this so much that he said, "This is a good place to stay. I'm tired of working so hard to find enough food to eat."

The eagle said, "This sounds fishy to me. There must be a catch in it. Besides, I like flying anywhere I want to go." So he flew away.

The chicken liked his new home very much. He didn't work any more. He just ate and got lazy. Then one day, he heard the farmer say that the preacher was coming to visit and they would have fried chicken for dinner.

The chicken said, "I must get out of here fast." But the chicken couldn't fly any more because he was too fat, soft, and out of practice. What do you think happened to the chicken?

You pay a high price for what you think is a "free lunch."

America

My country, 'tis of thee,
Sweet land of liberty,
    Of thee I sing.
Land where my fathers died,
Land of the pilgrims' pride,
From every mountain-side
    Let freedom ring.

Our fathers' God, to thee,
Author of liberty,
    To thee I sing.
Long may our land be bright
With freedom's holy light;
Protect us by Thy might,
    Great God, our King!

Samuel Francis Smith

Congratulations!

Now you can read big words

with five or more syllables:

hippopotamus

Tyrannosaurus Rex

cafeteria

refrigerator

planetarium

encyclopedia

consideration

Philadelphia

Learning the Sounds

A: alligator, apple, ant, ax, arrows, accident, acrobat, ambulance

U: umbrella, Uncle Sam, untied (shoe), underwear (or undressed), unbuttoned (shirt), upside down (turtle), umpire.

I: igloo, Indian, inner-tube, inchworm on an inch, iguana, ink, insect.

O: octopus, ostrich, olive, otter, ox.

E: envelope, elephant, elbow, eggs, elk, engine, eskimo.

M: mouth, mountain, moon, monkey, mittens, motorcycle, match, mouse.

S: sailboat, squirrel, sun, sandwich, soldier, soap, spider, Santa Claus.

R: ring, rabbit, rose, rocket, red, rain, rocking chair, rattlesnake.

P: peanut, pig, pumpkin, policeman, pie, pants, parrot, panda.

F: fish, fox, flag, foot, feather, fork, farm, fence.

D: doll, dog, dinosaur, duck, dollar, doughnut, door, deer.

G: goat, grasshopper, goal, guitar, green, gun, gorilla, gate.

T: telephone, tiger, tree, television, turkey, tent, turtle, teeth.

B: bicycle, bat and ball, bear, bananas, blue, boat, bed, basket.

N: necklace, nest, nose, nurse, nickel, newspaper, nail, nut.

C: cap, cat, cup, corn on the cob.

K: kite, king, key, kangaroo.

H: hair, horse, hat, ham, house, hand, hammer, helicopter.

L: ladder, lips, lion, leaf, leg, lemon, log, lock.

J: jacks, jar of jam or jelly, jelly beans, juggler, jug, jet plane, juice.

W: watch, worm, wagon, wallet.

Q: Queen, quacking duck, question mark, quarter.

V: vegetables, volcano, valentine.

X: six, ax

Y: yard, yellow yarn, yams.

Z: zipper, zoo, zebra.

Sh: ship, shell, sheep, shirt, shadow, shooting cannon, shoe, shoulder.

Ch: church, chair, chicken, chimpanzee, cheese, chain, chimney, cherries.

THE ORDER OF THE LESSONS

47.	ch, tch	71.	ar
48.	Sentences	72.	ur, ir, er
49.	sl, cl, bl	73.	or
50.	pl, fl, gl	74.	Ending: er
51.	sp, sc, sk, sn	75.	ee (bee)
52.	sm, sw, st, str	76.	ea (leaf)
53.	Sentences	77.	ai (train)
54.	Ending blends	78.	ay (day)
55.	a (cape)	79.	ie (pie), y (by)
56.	i (hide)	80.	oa (boat)
57.	u (cube), o (joke), e (Eve)	81.	ow (low), oe (toe)
58.	Sentences	82.	Review
59.	o (old), i (kind)	83.	ou (mouse)
60.	Ending: s	84.	ow (cow)
61.	tr, cr, fr	85.	ce, ci, cy (cent)
62.	dr, gr, br	86.	Sentences
63.	Sentences	87.	oi (coin), oy (boy)
64.	Sentences	88.	oo (moon, book)
65.	ng	89.	Sentences
66.	nk	90.	"The Goose and the Gold Eggs"
67.	th, wh	91.	ew (crew), ue (new)
68.	ing (clapping)	92.	al (ball)
69.	ing (making)	93.	"The Swing"
70.	Sentences	94.	aw (paw), au (Paul)

142. ou (dough, you, could, rough, ought); gh (laugh)

143. "Happy Thought"

144. "The Boy and the Wolf"

145. "Mary Had a Little Lamb"

146. "Twinkle, Twinkle, Little Star"

147. "All Things Bright and Beautiful"

148. "Humpty Dumpty," "Whole Duty of Children"

149. "Bed in Summer"

150. ear (earn), or (word), ei (eight), ch (Christmas), "The Owl"

151. "Time To Wake Up"

152. 3-syllable words

153. "Thirty Days," "Little Jack Horner"

154. 3-syllable words

155. "Ways to Go Places"

156. 3-syllable names

157. ei (receive), ove (move)

158. "The Wind," Disasters

159. tion (nation), sion (mansion), cian (musician)

160. sion (vision), sure (treasure), ture (picture), ous (joyous)

161. "Which One Loved Mother Best?"

162. 4-syllable words

163. "The Eagle and the Chicken"

164. "America"

165. 5-syllable words

Page Instructions for the Teacher

viii Have the child look at each of the ears and eyes and explain each one. You should refer to this Ears and Eyes page frequently. Pictures of **Ears** are used throughout *First Reader* to identify words that the child must sound out. Pictures of **Eyes** are used to identify words that we recognize by sight and do not sound out.

1. Have the child identify the **A** pictures: **a**lligator, **a**pple, **a**nt, **a**x, **a**rrows, **a**ccident, **a**crobat, **a**mbulance. Help him if he doesn't recognize any picture. Teach him to hear the **a** sound as it is heard in these words. Emphasize the **a** sound so the child hears it clearly. The child must learn to recognize and pronounce **a** like **a** in apple. Do **not** pronounce it like A in the ABCs. See if you and the child can think up any other words that start with **a**, as in apple.

Explain to the child that every letter can be written in two ways: a small letter and a big (or capital) letter. The small **a** is used most of the time, and the big **A** is used at the beginning of a sentence or for somebody's name (such as Andy or Ann). Have the child write the letters **A** and **a** with the fat pencil on the A pages in *First Reader Workbook*.

2. Have the child identify the **U** pictures: **u**mbrella, **U**ncle Sam, **u**ntied (shoe), **u**nderwear (or **u**ndressed), **u**nbuttoned (shirt), **u**pside down (turtle), **u**mpire. Teach him to hear the **u** sound as it is heard in these words. Emphasize the **u** sound. The child must learn that **U** and **u** sound like **u** in **u**mbrella and **not** like U in the alphabet.

Explain that the small **u** is used most of the time, and the big **U** is used for the start of a sentence or someone's name (such as Uncle Dan). Review the difference in sound between **a** and **u** and make sure the child pronounces the two sounds clearly and recognizes the sounds when you say them. Have the child write the letters **U** and **u** on the U pages with the fat pencil in the *Workbook*.

3. Have the child identify the **I** pictures: **i**gloo, **I**ndian, **i**nner-tube, **i**nchworm on an **i**nch (of the ruler), **i**guana, **i**nk, **i**nsect. Teach him to hear the **i** sound as it is heard in these words, **not** like I in the alphabet. The child must learn that **I** and **i** sound like **I** in **I**ndian.

Explain that the small **i** is used most of the time, and the big **I** is used for the start of a sentence or someone's name (such as **I**sabel). Review the difference in sound among **a**, **u**, **i**. Make sure the child clearly pronounces and recognizes the different sounds. Write the letters **I** and **i** on the I pages in the *Workbook*. Have the child trace the letters with his finger.

4. Have the child identify the **O** pictures: **o**ctopus, **o**strich, **o**live, **o**tter, **o**x. Teach the **o** as it is heard in these words, **not** like the letter O in the alphabet. Explain that the small **o** is used most of the time, and the big **O** for the start of a sentence or someone's name (such as **O**llie, **O**tto, or **O**scar).

Review the differences in sound among **A**, **U**, **I**, **O**. Make sure the child clearly pronounces and recognizes the

172

different sounds. Write the letters on the **O** pages in the *Workbook*. You can write **A**, **a**, **U**, **u**, **I**, **i**, **O**, **o** on large pieces of paper and put them around your home to help the child recognize them and pronounce them correctly.

5. Have the child identify the **E** pictures: **e**nvelope, **e**lephant, **e**lbow, **e**ggs, **e**lk, **e**ngine, **e**skimo. Teach the child to recognize the **e** as it is heard in these words, **not** like E in the alphabet. Explain that the small **e** is used most of the time, and the big **E** is used for the start of a sentence or someone's name (such as **E**ddie or **E**mily). Have the child write the letters on the **E** pages in the *Workbook*.

Review and practice the different sounds, **A**, **U**, **I**, **O**, **E**. These are the most important five pages in the book, and it is vital that the child pronounce and recognize these sounds when he sees and hears them. Many children find it difficult to learn the difference between **I** and **E**, so do extra practice in these sounds. Don't go forward in *First Reader* until the child knows these five sounds.

6. Have the child identify the **M** pictures: **m**outh, **m**ountain, **m**oon, **m**onkey, **m**ittens, **m**otorcycle, **m**atch, **m**ouse. Teach the child to recognize the **m** sound as it is heard at the beginning of each word (**not** as we say the letter M in the alphabet). Explain that the small **m** is used most of the time, and the big **M** is used at the start of a sentence or someone's name (such as **M**ary, **M**ichael, or **M**other). Continue writing each new letter in the *Workbook*.

7. Now we are ready to start combining **a**, **u**, **i**, **o**, **e** (which are called vowels)

with the other letters in the alphabet (which are called consonants). Teach the child how to combine the **m** sound with each of the vowels. Call attention to the picture of the **ear** at the top of the page. The ear means that the child should hear the sounds and connect them with the letters on the page. Say the sounds slowly and distinctly so the child will hear and say every letter as he reads the words, starting with **m-a-n**. Then combine the letters faster to say **man**.

Call attention to the picture of the **eye** in the middle of the page. The eye identifies words that do not follow regular rules, and so you just have to see them with your eye and memorize them. Let's call these "sight" or "eye" words. Be sure to read the sentences from left to right.

8. Identify the **S** pictures: **s**ailboat, **s**quirrel, **s**un, **s**andwich, **s**oldier, **s**oap, **s**pider, **S**anta Claus. Emphasize the **s** sound at the beginning of each word (**not** as we say the letter S in the alphabet). Point out the difference between the small **s** and the big **S**, which would be used for somebody's name (such as **S**arah).

9. Teach the child to combine the **s** sound with **a**, **u**, **i**, **o**, **e**. Call attention to the **ear** at the top of the page and help the child to hear every letter in the words and pronounce them correctly. Don't hurry; the child must go over and over these first pages until he knows them perfectly. Make sure the child is hearing and seeing the difference between the **si** words and the **se** words.

For all the columns of words in *First Reader*, the teacher should pronounce the word correctly **after** the child says it or tries to say it.

10. Identify the **R** pictures: **r**ing, **r**abbit, **r**ose, **r**ocket, the color **r**ed, **r**ain, **r**ocking chair, **r**attlesnake. Emphasize the **r** sound at the beginning of each word (**not** as we say R in the alphabet). Point out the difference between the small **r** and the big **R**.

11. Combine the **r** with the other sounds the child already knows. Don't hurry the child. He must hear and say every sound on the page perfectly. Call attention to the **ear** for the sounds you hear, and to the **eye** for the "sight" words that the child must recognize with his eye. Follow the same instructions given on the **m** and **s** pages.

12. Identify the **P** pictures: **p**eanut, **p**ig, **p**umpkin, **p**oliceman, **p**ie, **p**ants, **p**arrot, **p**anda. Emphasize the **p** sound in each word.

13. Combine **p** with the other sounds the child already knows in the same slow and careful way. Go over and over the words until the child reads them all perfectly. Call attention to the **eye** words. Reward the child when he reads the page perfectly.

14. Identify the **F** pictures: **f**ish, **f**ox, **f**lag, **f**oot, **f**eather, **f**ork, **f**arm, **f**ence. Teach the child to say the **f** sound distinctly for each word.

15. Combine **f** with the other sounds. Explain the difference between the **ear** and **eye** words. Continue with the same instructions given on previous pages.

16. Identify the **D** pictures: **d**oll, **d**og, **d**inosaur, **d**uck, **d**ollar, **d**oughnut, **d**oor, **d**eer.

17. Combine **d** with the other sounds. Teach the child to read the sentences with expression. Point out that a **period** marks the end of each sentence.

18. Identify the **G** pictures: **g**oat, **g**rasshopper, **g**oal, **g**uitar, the color **g**reen, **g**un, **g**orilla, **g**ate.

19. Combine **g** with the other sounds. In the second group of **ear** words, point out the **g** sound at the end of the words. Explain that a question mark is used at the end of a sentence that asks a question.

20. Identify the **T** pictures: **t**elephone, **t**iger, **t**ree, **t**elevision, **t**urkey, **t**ent, **t**urtle, **t**eeth.
Tell the child to point out household items that start with the **t** sound, as well as other sounds the child has already learned. Continue doing this with new sounds as the child learns them.

21. Combine **t** with the other sounds. When you teach the **eye** words, explain that quotation marks are used at the beginning and the end of what somebody actually says.

22. Identify the **B** pictures: **b**icycle, **b**at and **b**all, **b**ear, **b**ananas, the color **b**lue, **b**oat, **b**ed, **b**asket.

23. Combine **b** with the other sounds. Many children confuse the **b** and the **d** sounds, so this is a good time to review the **d** (on pages 16 and 17) and practice the difference. Point out the difference between the way the **b** and the **d** are written in the *Workbook*. Have the child trace **b** and **d** with his finger as well as with a pencil.

24. Identify the **N** pictures: **n**ecklace, **n**est, **n**ose, **n**urse, **n**ickel, **n**ewspaper, **n**ail, **n**ut.

25. Combine **n** with the other sounds. Point out the words that end in the **n** sound.

26. Identify the **C** pictures: **c**ap, **c**at, **c**up, **c**orn on the **c**ob. Identify the **K** pictures: **k**ite, **k**ing, **k**ey, **k**angaroo. Explain that **C** and **K** have the same sound.

27. Combine the **c** with the **a**, **u**, and **o** words, and combine the **k** with the **i** and **e** words. Explain that **ck** at the end of words has the same sound.

28. Now we can read more sentences! Help the child to say every sound in every word in every sentence, and read the sentences with enthusiasm, left to right.

29. This is a review page where all the sounds are in a different order. Make it a challenge to the child to see if he can read them correctly. Reward him if he does. The **eye** words at the bottom of the page are review words, too. They must be memorized.

30. Identify the **H** pictures: **h**air, **h**orse, **h**at, **h**am, **h**ouse, **h**and, **h**ammer, **h**elicopter.

31. Combine **h** with the other sounds and be sure the child hears the **h** sound in the sentences.

32. Identify the **L** pictures: **l**adder, **l**ips, **l**ion, **l**eaf, **l**eg, **l**emon, **l**og, **l**ock.

33. Combine the **l** with the other sounds. Sound out the second set of **ear** words with the **l** sound at the end. Don't forget to explain the difference between the small **l** and the big **L** used for people's names (such as **L**arry).

34. Identify the **J** pictures: **j**acks, **j**ar of **j**am or **j**elly, **j**elly beans, **j**uggler, **j**ug, **j**et plane, **j**uice.

35. Combine **j** with the other sounds. Learn the **eye** words. Have the child read the sentences with enthusiasm.

36. Identify the **W** pictures: **w**atch, **w**orm, **w**agon, **w**allet. Then identify the **Q** pictures: **q**ueen, **q**uacking duck, **q**uestion mark, **q**uarter. Note that **q** usually appears as **qu**.

37. Combine **w** with the other sounds, and then combine **qu** with the other sounds.

38. Identify the **V** pictures: **v**egetables, **v**olcano, **v**alentine. Then identify the **X** pictures and note that the **x** comes at the end of the word: si**x**, a**x**.

39. Combine **v** with the other sounds, and then combine **x** with the other sounds.

40. Identify the **Y** pictures: **y**ard, **y**ellow **y**arn, **y**ams. Then identify the **Z** pictures: **z**ipper, **z**oo, **z**ebra.

41. Combine **y** with the other sounds, and then combine **z** with the other sounds.

42. This page combines two consonants at the end of a word. Teach the child to say the words slowly and carefully, hearing every letter. Then, say the words faster so that the two sounds blend together.

Explain that the apostrophe in the names in the right-hand column is used when something belongs to someone (as in Tom's book).

43. This is a review page. Give the child a challenge to see if he can read the words when they appear in a different order. The **eye** words are also a review. Reward the child when he can read the page perfectly.

44. Identify the **sh** pictures: **sh**ip, **sh**ell, **sh**eep, **sh**irt, **sh**adow, **sh**ooting cannon, **sh**oe, **sh**oulder. Explain the difference in the sound between **sh** and **s** on page 8.

45. Combine **sh** with the other sounds. Note that the second set of **ear** words has the **sh** sound at the end of the word.

46. Identify the **ch** pictures: **ch**urch, **ch**air, **ch**icken, **ch**impanzee, **ch**eese, **ch**ain, **ch**imney, **ch**erries. Explain the difference between the **ch** and the **sh** sounds.

47. Combine **ch** with the other sounds. Explain that **ch** can come at the beginning or end of a word. Sometimes this sound is written **tch**.

48. The child should feel a sense of accomplishment when he reads sentences with so many different sounds. Be sure you read the sentences from left to right.

49. Now we are ready to blend two sounds at the start of a word: **sl** as in

sled, **cl** as in **cl**ock, **bl** as in **bl**ack. Help the child to blend sounds he has already learned in order to make new words.

50. More beginning blends: **pl** as in **pl**um, **fl** as in **fl**ash, **gl** as in **gl**ad.

51. More beginning blends: **sp** as in **sp**in, **sc** as in **sc**at, **sk** as in **sk**in, **sn** as in **sn**ap.

52. More beginning blends: **sm** as in **Sm**ith, **sw** as in **sw**im, **st** as in **st**ick, **str** as in **str**uck. Note that **str** combines three sounds to start a word.

53. The **eye** words at the top just have to be learned. Now the child can read many words with different blends of sounds and letters! He is learning how to put sounds together like building blocks in order to read new words.

54. Letter blends can be combined at the end of a word, too. Have the child pronounce each word slowly and carefully in order to hear every letter, and then say the words faster so the blends combine properly. Review the **eye** words at the bottom of the page.

55. Up to this point, we have learned a certain sound for the five vowels: **a, u, i, o, e.** We call the sounds we have already learned the **short** vowels. Now, we are going to learn how the sound of these vowels can change.

When the letter **e** is added at the end of a word, you don't hear that **e,** but it changes the sound to what we call the **long** vowel. The **long** vowel sound is the way the five vowels sound when you recite your ABCs. These new words are **ear** words, too, but the sound is different so you have to listen more closely. That's why the picture at the top of the page shows a child with his hand behind his ear. We learn how the letter **e** at the end of a word changes the **short a** to a **long a**. See how adding the letter **e** changes c**a**p to c**a**pe, and changes c**a**n to c**a**ne.

56. Listen closely! Another hand has brought the letter **e** to add to the end of some **i** words, and it changes the sound from a **short i** to a **long i**. See how the **short i** in h**i**d changes to the **long i** in h**i**de, and the **short i** in k**i**t changes to the **long i** in k**i**te.

57. Here's another hand bringing the letter **e**. You don't hear the letter **e**, but see how that letter **e** changes the **short u** to the **long u**, and changes the **short o** to the **long o**, and changes the **short e** to the **long e**. For example, see how c**u**b changes to c**u**be, and r**o**d changes to r**o**de. See how the names Eve and Steve have the **long e** sound because of the **e** at the end of the word.

58. Now you can read many new words using both **short** vowels and **long** vowels. Be sure to praise the child when he can read the sentences all by himself.

59. Some words don't follow the rule. They have the **long** vowel sound, but they just don't have that letter **e** at the end. That's why the **e** is crossed out at the top of the page. Let's see if you can read these words with the **long** vowel sound anyway, such as **old**.

60. Many words end in the **s** sound. Pronounce the words slowly so you can hear every letter, then faster to make the blends smooth at the end of the words.

61. Here are some more beginning blends: **tr** as in **tr**uck, **cr** as in **cr**ack, **fr** as in **Fr**ank. Speak them slowly at first, to make sure that the child hears every letter. Then, say the words faster, being sure that the child says the blends correctly.

62. More beginning blends: **dr** as in **dr**um, **gr** as in **gr**ab, **br** as in **br**ush.

63. Study the **eye** words. Then have the child read the sentences using all the new blends we have learned.

64. More beginning blends and more sentences to practice them.

65. Here are the **ng** words. Do you want to si**ng**? Or to ri**ng** bells? If so, you have to know the **ng** words.

66. Here are the **nk** words. They are sort of fun to say, don't you think?

67. You have to listen very closely when you say the **th** and the **wh** words. For the first group of **th** words, you have to put your tongue up against your front teeth and blow a little air through them, as in **th**anks.

In the second group of **th** words, **th** is very quiet and you don't hear any air pushing through your teeth, as in **th**em.

For the **wh** words, you have to blow a little air through your teeth, as in **wh**ale. Do you hear the difference between the **wh** words like **wh**ich, and the **w** words like **w**itch?

68. You can make a lot of new words by adding **ing** to words you already know. If the word has a **short** vowel in it, we usually add another consonant before we add the **ing**, as in clap**ping** or nap**ping**.

69. **But**, when we add **ing** to words with a **long** vowel, we drop the extra **e** but we keep the long vowel sound. In the word hid, we hear the **short i**. When we add the letter **e**, hid changes to hide and we hear the **long i**. When we add **ing** to hide, we drop that extra **e,** but we keep the **long i** sound and the word is hiding.

70. This is a page where you can read some words with the new **ear** sounds you have learned. The **eye** words are important, too, so practice saying them until you know them. Then, you can read the sentences.

71. **R** is a letter that changes the sound of vowels in a different way, so listen closely. When **a** is followed by **r**, it makes an **ar** word like c**ar** and sh**ar**k. Now read the page with lots of **ar** words.

72. When **u, i,** or **e** is followed by **r**, it makes the sound you hear in b**ur**n; **ur**, **ir**, and **er** all sound like **ur** in b**ur**n.

73. When **o** is followed by **r**, it makes an **or** word that sounds like h**or**se.

74. A lot of words end in **er**. These words are easy to read; you just add **er** on the end of the word.

75. On this page, we learn the **ee**. It has a **long e** sound like bumble b**ee** and h**ee**l. At the bottom of the page are some **eye** words that have only one **e** (like m**e** and h**e**), but they still have the **long e** sound. One funny **ee** word is different: been is pronounced "bin."

76. The letters **ea** usually have a **long e** sound like **ee**, as in l**ea**f.

77. The letters **ai** sound like a **long a**, as in tr**ai**n. But one funny **ai** word is different: again is pronounced to rhyme with "the men."

78. The letters **ay** sound like a **long a**, as in pr**ay** and d**ay**.

79. The letters **ie** sound like a **long i**, as in p**ie** and t**ie**. When **y** comes at the end of a word, it also sounds like a **long i**, as in cr**y** and tr**y**.

80. The letters **oa** sound like a **long o**, as in b**oa**t and c**oa**t.

81. The letters **ow** sound like a **long o**, as in l**ow** and sh**ow**. The letters **oe** also sound like a **long o**, as in t**oe** and J**oe**.

82. This is a review page to see how well the child has learned some of the **ear** and **eye** words. Be sure to praise the child when he reads the page perfectly.

83. The letters **ou** make the sound we hear in m**ou**se and h**ou**se.

84. The letters **ow** also have a different sound from the one we learned on page 81. The letters **ow** can also sound like c**ow** and cl**ow**n. It is the same sound as **ou** in m**ou**se.

85. Listen for a new sound of the letter **c**, called the **soft c**. When **c** is followed by **e** or **i** or **y**, it sounds like an **s**, as in i**c**e cubes.

86. Now let's try some harder words with the **soft c**, and also a few more **eye**

words. We need the **soft c** for important words like i**c**e cream and bi**c**ycle. Note that bi**c**y**c**le uses both the soft c and the hard c.

87. The letters **oi** and **oy** make a very different sound, like c**oi**n and j**oi**n, and like b**oy** and j**oy**.

88. The letters **oo** have two different sounds. The **oo** words at the top of the page sound like m**oo**n and z**oo**. The **oo** words at the bottom of the page sound like b**oo**k and f**oo**t. Do you hear the difference?

89. See how many sentences you can read using both kinds of **oo** words.

90. Now you can read a whole story!

91. Sometimes letters are written one way, but we pronounce them another way. On this page, your **eye** sees the letters **ew** and **ue**, but your **ear** must hear them like **oo**. Read the words like cr**ew** and bl**ue** with the **oo** sound.

The **ew** words in the middle of the page also have the **oo** sound, but it is slightly different — they rhyme with "you."

92. Another letter that changes the sound of **a** is the letter **l**. When **l** follows **a**, the word sounds like b**all** or s**alt**.

93. Now you can read a famous poem. Do you hear the rhymes at the end of each line?

94. The letters **aw** sound like p**aw** and s**aw**. The letters **au** have the same sound, like P**au**l and M**au**d.

95. On this page, we learn that the letters **ea** have another sound that is different from the sound we learned on page 76. **Ea** is sometimes pronounced **ea**, as in br**ea**d.

The letters **ie** can also have another sound that is different from the sound we learned on page 79; **ie** sometimes has the **long e** sound, like ch**ie**f and th**ie**f.

96. In the story about the little red hen, look for words with **ou**, **oo**, **ing**, **ea**, **oa**, **ow**, and **ee**.

97. Do you hear the rhymes at the end of each line?

98. Read the poem about the shadow. Look for the **ow** words.

99. In the story about the rabbit and the turtle, look for the **oa**, **au**, **ea**, **ce**, **aw**, and **ee** words.

100. In the poem about the wind and the leaves, look for words with **ea**, **ay**, **ow**, **ou**, and **ew**.

101. It's easy to add a quick **a** in front of words you already know, as in **a**wake.

102. Here we learn lots of **wh** words. Some are **ear** words with short vowels. Others don't follow any rule, so they are **eye** words and you just have to learn them. Listen for the difference between **wh** and just **w**, as in **wh**ether and **w**eather.

103. With your eye, you see the letters **se**, but sometimes they sound like **z**, as in ro**se** and no**se**. Plea**se** is a very important word you should know.

104. It is easy to add **y** or **ie** to the end of words you already know, as in bell**y**, jell**y**, kitt**ies**, part**ies**.

105. In the story about the fox and the crow, look for words with **ie**, **ee**, **ea**, **ce**, **se**, **ai**, and **ou**.

106. Let's practice some **y** and **ie** words.

107. Can you read the poems?

108. Here are some beginning **r** blends: **thr** as in **thr**ead, **scr** as in **scr**ape, **spr** as in **spr**ing, **str** as in **str**ing.

109. With your eye, you see the letters **ge** or **dge**, but you must pronounce them and hear them like **j**, as in ca**ge** and p**age**.

110. Practice sentences with the **ge** sound. Learn the difference between three words that sound the same — but have different spellings and different meanings. Review some **eye** words at the bottom of the page.

111. In the story about the grasshopper, look for the words with **ai**, **ea**, **ar**, **al**, **ou**, and **ing**.

112. Some words end in **el** like nick**el**, and they sound just as you expect them to sound. Some words end in **le**, but you should say them and hear them just like the **el** words, as in ratt**le**.

113. Some words end in **or**, but you should hear them as though they end in **er**, like mirr**or** and doct**or**.

114. In the story about the dog and his bone, look for the words with **dge**, **oo**, **ar**, and **ou**.

115. A lot of words end in **ed**. It should be easy for you to add that sound, as in tast**ed**.

116. See if you can find all the words that end in **ed**.

117. Sometimes, words that end in **ed** sound as if they just ended in **d**, as in rain**ed**.

118. These sentences have both kinds of **ed** endings. Can you read them correctly?

119. Sometimes you see the **ed** on the end of a word, but you hear it like **t,** as in stopp**ed**.

120. Here are some more **ed** words that sound as if they end in **t**, such as march**ed**.

121. Here are some important **eye** words, and sentences with all three kinds of **ed** endings.

122. Now you can put so many sounds together and read two-syllable words.

123. In the story about the milkmaid, sound out the words with two syllables.

124. Here are lots of two-syllable words to read.

125. In the story about the cat and the mice, look for the words with **ai**, **ce**, **ee**, **ou**, **wh**, and with two syllables.

126. More two-syllable words to read.

127. In the story about the wind and the sun, look for the words with **oa**, **er**, and **ou**.

128. This is a page of names of girls and boys. Do you know anybody with these names?

129. You learned about the **ar** words on page 71. Now we put the letter **e** after **ar** words and get the sound of fl**are** and b**are**. The **air** words, such as st**air**s and h**air**, have the same sound.

130. Some words have letters that you do not say or hear at all. You can see the letters **gh**, but you don't say them at all. That's why your hands are covering your ears.

131. In the story about the lion and the mouse, look for the words with **ou**, **aw**, **ee**, **ea**, **ow**, **au**, **ew**, and the silent **gh**.

132. You see the letters **ove**, but you pronounce them **uv**, as in l**ove**.

133. Sometimes you see the letters **on**, but instead of saying **on**, you pronounce them **un**, as in son, or **wun**, as in the number one.

134. Learn your numbers. Can you read the words with the silent **gh**?

135. Here are more silent letters. You see the **b**, **k**, **t**, and **w**, but you do not say or hear them. That's why your hands are covering your ears for words such as lam**b**, **k**not, lis**t**en, and **w**rap.

136. Here are more silent letters. You see the **u**, **h**, and **l**, but you do not say or hear them, as in b**u**ild, Jo**h**n, ta**l**k.

137. See if you can read the poem perfectly.

138. Read the story about the donkey who tried to be a lion. See if you can spot all the silent **gh** words.

139. Read the poem and listen for the rhymes.

140. You see the letters **ph**, but you hear them like **f**, as in **ph**one and ele**ph**ant.

141. Read the story about the eagle and the turtle. Look for the words with **oa**, **aw**, **ou**, **ea**, **ow**, **ie**, and **tch**. Find the words with the silent letters.

142. The letters **ou** have five different sounds (in addition to the one we learned on page 83). These five new sounds rhyme with doe, moon, book, cuff, and paw.

   At the bottom of the page is a special sound for **gh**. Usually those letters are silent, but sometimes they sound like **f**, as in lau**gh**.

143. Reading can be a lot of fun! Which poem do you like best?

144. Read the story about the boy and the wolf.

145. Read the poem about Mary and her little lamb.

146. Twinkle, twinkle is a famous poem.

147. Read about our beautiful world.

148. You are learning to read about so many different things.

149. Another poem.

150. Here are letters that you see one way with your **eye**, but they have a different sound when you say them. The letters **ear** and **or** sometimes sound like **ur**, as in l**ear**n or w**or**m.

The letters **ei** and **eigh** sometimes sound like **ay**, as in **eigh**t. The letters **ch** sometimes have a **hard ch** sound like **k**, as in **Ch**ristmas.

151. Time to wake up!

152. Now you can read three-syllable words.

153. More poems to read.

154. Can you read all the three-syllable words?

155. How many ways to travel can you name?

156. Here are some girls' and boys' names with three syllables. Do you know anybody with these names?

157. The letters **ei** sound like **ee**, as in rec**ei**ve. The letters **ove** have another

sound (from the sound we learned on page 132). Sometimes you hear them like **oove**, as in m**ove**. In the middle of the page are a few more **eye** words to learn.

158. Read a poem about the wind and some weather words.

159. When you see the letters **tion**, **sion**, **cian**, and **tian**, you should hear and pronounce them like **shun**, as in na**tion**, vaca**tion**, musi**cian**.

160. Here are more syllables that are written one way, but you hear and pronounce them another way. We see **sion**, but we hear **zhun**, as in televi**sion**. We see **sure**, but we hear **zhur**, as in trea**sure**. We see **ture**, but we hear **chur**, as in pic**ture**. We see **ous**, but we hear **us**, as in fam**ous**.

161. Read the poem.

162. Now you can read four-syllable words! Sound out each syllable carefully.

163. Read about the eagle and the chicken.

164. Read about America. Maybe you can sing it, too.

165. Now you can sound out five-syllable words. You can read!

Note: When we refer to the child as "he," we mean both boys and girls.

Afterword

After you have learned all the sounds and syllables in *First Reader*, you are now ready to read more stories and books. When you come across a word that doesn't sound right when you try to sound it out, be sure to ask someone else for help, or consult a dictionary for the meaning and pronunciation. A few words in the English language don't follow regular rules, so you just have to learn them.

To find interesting stories and books to read, go to a library and ask the librarian to find books for the second and third grade levels that were published **before** 1970. To find out **when** a book was published, first find the Title Page, which is in the front of every book. Then look on the back side of the Title Page. Somewhere in the fine print, you will find the date that the book was first published.

There are hundreds of good books you can now read, and the best ones were published **before** 1970. Tell the librarian what subjects you like to read about. You can also find good books at book fairs and other sales of used books.

I wish you the Joy of Reading! You are on your way to a good education, because now you will be able to read the great books written in the English language.

Phyllis Schlafly